H. C. Bunner

The Poems of H.C. Bunner

H. C. Bunner
The Poems of H.C. Bunner
ISBN/EAN: 9783744710817
Printed in Europe, USA, Canada, Australia, Japan
Cover: Foto ©Thomas Meinert / pixelio.de

More available books at **www.hansebooks.com**

THE POEMS OF H. C. BUNNER

> *A Book of Verses underneath the Bough,*
> *A Jug of Wine, a Loaf of Bread, and Thou*
> *Beside me singing in the Wilderness—*
> *Oh, Wilderness were Paradise enow!*
> —*Omar Khayyám*

NEW EDITION

NEW YORK
CHARLES SCRIBNER'S SONS
1899

INTRODUCTION

H. C. Bunner — for such was the signature Henry Cuyler Bunner chose to employ both in public and in private — was born at Oswego, N. Y., August 3, 1855, and he died at Nutley, N. J., May 11, 1896. His life was spent in the city of New York or in its immediate vicinity. Here he went to school; here he prepared for Columbia College, which he was regretfully unable to enter; here he worked for a while in a mercantile office; and here at last he was able to adopt the profession of letters. Here he wrote plays and stories and verses; and here he was for nearly a score of years the editor of *Puck*, the first comic journal to establish itself in America.

His work as a political journalist was as different as possible from most work done in that thorny field; it was vigorous but never violent. He sought to convince by sheer force of argument, and he tried always to be fair toward his opponents. But interest in the work of the journalist fades in a day or a week, or a month at most; while the story-teller and the poet are more fortunate, and their work may survive for a year or a decade, or a century if a single story, however brief, or a single lyric, however slight, has found a lodging in the hearts of the people. It is perhaps as a poet that the author of "Airs from Arcady" is likely longest to be remembered; and it is as a poet that he would have chosen to be cherished in men's memories. And his verse met with the same good fortune that befell his fiction; it pleased both the critical and the uncritical. It has the form, the finish, the flavor of scholarship that the cultivated recognize and relish; and it has also the freshness, the spontaneity, the heartiness, and the human sympathy wanting which no poetry has ever been welcome outside the narrow circle of the dilettanti.

In the present volume are included the contents of the two books of verse he published during his lifetime, "Airs from Arcady" in 1884, and "Rowen" in 1892, and also a selection from the "Ballads of the Town" (which he had been contributing to *Puck* for half-a-dozen years), together with a few of his later lyrics and the virile and resonant lines read before the Army of the Potomac at New London in 1895.

BRANDER MATTHEWS.

Columbia University.

CONTENTS

AIRS FROM ARCADY

	PAGE
INTRODUCTION	v
DEDICATION—To B. M.	xv

ARCADIA

The Way to Arcady	3
O Honey of Hymettus Hill	8
Daphnis	9
The Hour of Shadows	11
Robin's Song	12
A Lost Child	14

PHILISTIA

Da Capo	19
Gone	22
Just a Love-Letter	23
She was a Beauty	27
Candor	28
"Accepted"	30

CONTENTS

BOHEMIA

	PAGE
A Pitcher of Mignonette	35
Poetry and the Poet	36
Yes?	38
A Poem in the Programme	40
Betrothed	41
Dead in Bohemia — Irwin Russell	46

ELSEWHERE

Holiday Home	49
Forfeits	50
In School Hours	51
The Wail of the "Personally Conducted"	55
A Campaign Torch	57
Home, Sweet Home, with Variations. I.	60
II.—Swinburne	61
III.—Bret Harte	63
IV.—Horace—Austin Dobson	66
V.—Goldsmith—Pope	67
VI.—Walt Whitman	68

ULTIMA THULE

Forty	77
Strong as Death	80
Deaf	82
Les Morts vont Vite	83
Disaster	84
September	86
Then	87

CONTENTS

	PAGE
The Appeal to Harold	88
To a Dead Woman	91
The Old Flag	92
From a Counting-House	94
To a Hyacinth Plucked for Decoration Day	95
Longfellow	96
For the First Page of the Album	98
Farewell to Salvini	99
On Reading a Poet's First Book	100
Feminine	102
Redemption	103
Triumph	104
To Her	106

ROWEN

DEDICATION — To A. L. B.	109
At the Centennial Ball — 1889	113
The Last of the New Year's Callers	125
May-Bloom	127
The Linnet	129
Heave Ho!	130
An Old-Fashioned Love-Song	132
A Look Back	134
Prudence, Spinning	136
The Light	138
Grant	141
"Let Us Have Peace"	144
The Battle of Apia Bay	146
Wilhelm I., Emperor of Germany	148
General Sherman	152

CONTENTS

	PAGE
LEOPOLD DAMROSCH	155
J. B.	156
MY SHAKSPERE	159
ON SEEING MAURICE LELOIR'S ILLUSTRATIONS TO STERNE'S "SENTIMENTAL JOURNEY"	162
TO A READER OF THE XXIST CENTURY	163
FOR AN OLD POET	167
WILKIE COLLINS	168
FOR C. J. T., CONCERNING A. D.	170
EDMUND CLARENCE STEDMAN	171
AN EPISTLE	172
ON READING CERTAIN PUBLISHED LETTERS OF W. M. T.	175
CHAKEY EINSTEIN	179
A FABLE FOR RULERS	185
BISMARCK SOLILOQUIZES	186
IMITATION	190
"MAGDALENA"	191
"ONE, TWO, THREE!"	197
THE LITTLE SHOP	200
GRANDFATHER WATTS'S PRIVATE FOURTH	203
TO MY DAUGHTER	206
SCHUBERT'S KINDER-SCENEN	208

BALLADS OF THE TOWN AND LATER LYRICS

BALLADS OF THE TOWN

I.—THE MAID OF MURRAY HILL	215
II.—THE FRIVOLOUS GIRL	217
III.—KITTY'S SUMMERING	219

CONTENTS

	PAGE
IV.—At Dancing School	221
V.—Their Wedding Journey, 1834	224
VI.—To a June Breeze	227
VII.—The Chaperon	230
VIII.—A Song of Bedford Street	232

LATER LYRICS

The Red Box at Vesey Street	237
Shriven, A. D. 1425	240
Song for Labor Day	242
An Old Song	244
Unaware	246
The Quest	247
Lutetia	248
The Heart of the Tree	249
"They also Serve"	251
Notes	261

AIRS FROM ARCADY

AND ELSEWHERE

[1884]

TO BRANDER MATTHEWS:

'BY THE HEARTH

The night is late; your fire is whitening fast,
   Our speech has silent spaces, and is low;
   Yet there is much to say before I go —
And much is left unsaid, dear friend, at last.

Yet something may be said. This fading fire
   Was never cold for me; and never cold
   Has been the welcoming glance I knew of old —
Warm with a friendship usage could not tire.

The kindly hand has never failed me yet,
   And never yet has failed the cheering word;
   Nor ever went Perplexity unheard,
But ever was by thoughtful Counsel met.

The plans we made, the hopes we nursed, have fed
   These friendly embers with a genial fire.
   Not till my spirit ceases to aspire
Shall their kind light within my heart be dead.

Take these, the gathered songs of striving years,
   And many fledged and warmed beside your hearth;
   Not for whatever they may have of worth —
A simpler tie, perchance, my work endears.

With them this wish: that when your days shall close,
   Life, a well-used and well-contented guest,
   May gently press the hand I oft have pressed,
And leave you by Love's fire to calm repose.

ARCADIA

THE WAY TO ARCADY

OH, what's the way to Arcady,
  To Arcady, to Arcady;
Oh, what's the way to Arcady,
  Where all the leaves are merry?

Oh, what's the way to Arcady?
The spring is rustling in the tree—
The tree the wind is blowing through—
  It sets the blossoms flickering white.
I knew not skies could burn so blue
  Nor any breezes blow so light.
They blow an old-time way for me,
Across the world to Arcady.

Oh, what's the way to Arcady?
Sir Poet, with the rusty coat,
Quit mocking of the song-bird's note.

ARCADIA

How have you heart for any tune,
You with the wayworn russet shoon?
Your scrip, a-swinging by your side,
Gapes with a gaunt mouth hungry-wide.
I'll brim it well with pieces red,
If you will tell the way to tread.

*Oh, I am bound for Arcady,
And if you but keep pace with me
You tread the way to Arcady.*

And where away lies Arcady,
And how long yet may the journey be?

Ah, that (quoth he) *I do not know—
Across the clover and the snow—
Across the frost, across the flowers—
Through summer seconds and winter hours.
I've trod the way my whole life long,
  And know not now where it may be;
My guide is but the stir to song,
That tells me I can not go wrong,
  Or clear or dark the pathway be
  Upon the road to Arcady.*

ARCADIA

But how shall I do who can not sing?
  I was wont to sing, once on a time——
There is never an echo now to ring
  Remembrance back to the trick of rhyme.

'T is strange you cannot sing (quoth he),
The folk all sing in Arcady.

But how may he find Arcady
Who hath nor youth nor melody?

What, know you not, old man (quoth he)——
  Your hair is white, your face is wise—
  That Love must kiss that Mortal's eyes
Who hopes to see fair Arcady?
No gold can buy you entrance there;
But beggared Love may go all bare—
No wisdom won with weariness;
But Love goes in with Folly's dress—
No fame that wit could ever win;
But only Love may lead Love in
  To Arcady, to Arcady.

Ah, woe is me, through all my days
  Wisdom and wealth I both have got,
And fame and name, and great men's praise;
  But Love, ah, Love! I have it not.

ARCADIA

There was a time, when life was new —
  But far away, and half forgot —
I only know her eyes were blue;
  But Love — I fear I knew it not.
We did not wed, for lack of gold,
And she is dead, and I am old.
All things have come since then to me,
Save Love, ah, Love! and Arcady.

Ah, then I fear we part (quoth he),
My way's for Love and Arcady.

But you, you fare alone, like me;
  The gray is likewise in your hair.
  What love have you to lead you there,
To Arcady, to Arcady?

Ah, no, not lonely do I fare;
  My true companion's Memory.
With Love he fills the Spring-time air;
  With Love he clothes the Winter tree.
Oh, past this poor horizon's bound
  My song goes straight to one who stands —
Her face all gladdening at the sound —
  To lead me to the Spring-green lands,
To wander with enlacing hands.

ARCADIA

*The songs within my breast that stir
Are all of her, are all of her.
My maid is dead long years* (quoth he),
She waits for me in Arcady.

*Oh, yon's the way to Arcady,
  To Arcady, to Arcady;
Oh, yon's the way to Arcady,
  Where all the leaves are merry.*

O HONEY OF HYMETTUS HILL

RONDEL

[Dobson's Variation]

O HONEY of Hymettus Hill,
  Gold-brown, and cloying sweet to taste,
Wert here for the soft amorous bill
  Of Aphrodite's courser placed?

  Thy musky scent what virginal chaste
Blossom was ravished to distill,
O honey of Hymettus Hill,
  Gold-brown, and cloying sweet to taste?

What upturned calyx drank its fill
  When ran the draught divine to waste,
That her white hands were doomed to spill —
  Sweet Hebe, fallen and disgraced —
O honey of Hymettus Hill,
  Gold-brown, and cloying sweet to taste?

DAPHNIS

I

ERE the spring comes, we will go
Where belated lines of snow
Lie in wreathlets chilly bright
Round the wind-flowers pink and white,
Trembling even as you, my own,
In my arms about you thrown;
Where pale sheets of ice like glass
Fleck the marshland's greening grass;
Where beneath the budding trees
Dead leaves wait for April's breeze —
Chloë, Chloë, we will wander
Hither, thither, here and yonder.
Seeing you, the jealous Spring
Sure will haste a laggard wing,
  Though the upland plains are snowy,
Though the snow is on the plain —
  Chloë, Chloë, Chloë, Chloë!
But she answers not again.

ARCADIA

II

Chloë, lo! the Spring is here,
All the wintry walks are clear;
Prismy purple is the air
Round the branches brown and bare;
Purple are the doubtful dyes
Of the clouds in April's skies —
Come, and make last Summer stretch
Over half a year, and fetch
Smells of rose and violet
In the barren ways to set.
See, the wood remembering misses
Sweetness of our last year's kisses.
O'er the place where once we kist
Falls a vail of rainy mist —
 Tangled rain-sheets, wreathed and blowy —
There is weeping in the rain —
 Chloë, Chloë, Chloë, Chloë!
Ah! she answers not again!

THE HOUR OF SHADOWS [1]

UPON that quiet day that lies
  Where forest branches screen the skies,
The spirit of the eve has laid
A deeper and a dreamier shade;
And winds that through the tree-tops blow
Wake not the silent gloom below.

Only the sound of far-off streams,
Faint as our dreams of childhood's dreams,
Wandering in tangled pathways crost,
Like woodland truants strayed and lost,
Their faint, complaining echoes roam,
Threading the forest toward their home.

O brooks, I too have gone astray,
And left my comrade on the way —
Guide me through aisles where soft you moan
To some sad spot you know alone,
Where only leaves and nestlings stir,
And I may dream, and dream of Her.

ROBIN'S SONG

Warwickshire, 16—

Up, up, my heart! up, up, my heart,
  This day was made for thee!
For soon the hawthorn spray shall part,
  And thou a face shalt see
That comes, O heart, O foolish heart,
  This way to gladden thee.

The grass shows fresher on the way
  That soon her feet shall tread—
The last year's leaflet curled and gray,
  I could have sworn was dead,
Looks green, for lying in the way
  I know her feet will tread.

ARCADIA

What hand yon blossom curtain stirs,
   More light than errant air?
I know the touch—'tis hers, 'tis hers!
   She parts the thicket there—
The flowerèd branch her coming stirs
   Hath perfumed all the air.

The Springs of all forgotten years
   Are waked to life anew—
Up, up, my eyes, nor fill with tears
   As tender as the dew—
I knew her not in all those years;
   But life begins anew.

Up, up, my heart! up, up, my heart,
   This daý was made for thee!
Come, Wit, take on thy nimblest art,
   And win Love's victory—
What now? Where art thou, coward heart?
   Thy hour is here—and She!

A LOST CHILD

Yᴇ CRYER

HERE'S a reward for who'll find Love
  Love is a-straying
  Ever since Maying,
Hither and yon, below, above;
  All are seeking Love!

Yᴇ HAND-BILL

Gone astray—between the Maying
  And the gathering of the hay,
LOVE, an urchin ever playing—
  Folk are warned against his play.

How may you know him? By the quiver,
  By the bow he's wont to bear.
First on your left there comes a shiver,
  Then a twinge — the arrow's there.

ARCADIA

By his eye of pansy color,
  Deep as wounds he dealeth free;
If its hue have faded duller,
  'T is not that he weeps for me.

By the smile that curls his mouthlet;
  By the mockery of his sigh;
By his breath, a spicy South, let
  Slip his lips of roses by.

By the devil in his dimple;
  By his lies that sound so true;
By his shaft-sting, that no simple
  Ever culled will heal for you.

By his beckonings that embolden;
  By his quick withdrawings then;
By his flying hair, a golden
  Light to lure the feet of men.

By the breast where ne'er a hurt'll
  Rankle 'neath his kerchief hid —
What? you cry; *he wore a kirtle?*
  Faith! methinks the rascal did!

ARCADIA

Here's a reward for who'll find Love!
Love is a-straying
Ever since Maying;
Hither and yon, below, above,
I am seeking Love.

Cryer: H. Bunner:
  Grub Street:
Cry's Weddings:
Buryings: Loft
Childⁿ, and right
cheaplie.
Ye IId Knocker.

     Master Corydon,

ye Finder pray'd
to Bring he₁ to

Petticoat Lane

PHILISTIA

DA CAPO

SHORT and sweet, and we 've come to the end of it—
   Our poor little love lying cold.
Shall no sonnet, then, ever be penned of it?
   Nor the joys and pains of it told?
How fair was its face in the morning,
   How close its caresses at noon,
How its evening grew chill without warning,
         Unpleasantly soon!

I can't say just how we began it—
   In a blush, or a smile, or a sigh;
Fate took but an instant to plan it;
   It needs but a moment to die.
Yet—remember that first conversation,
   When the flowers you had dropped at your feet
I restored. The familiar quotation
         Was—"Sweets to the sweet."

PHILISTIA

Oh, their delicate perfume has haunted
   My senses a whole season through.
If there *was* one soft charm that you wanted
   The violets lent it to you.
I whispered you, life was but lonely:
   A cue which you graciously took;
And your eyes learned a look for me only—
     A very nice look.

And sometimes your hand would touch *my* hand,
   With a sweetly particular touch;
You said many things in a sigh, and
   Made a look express wondrously much.
We smiled for the mere sake of smiling,
   And laughed for no reason but fun;
Irrational joys; but beguiling—
     And all that is done!

We were idle, and played for a moment
   At a game that now neither will press:
I cared not to find out what "No" meant;
   Nor your lips to grow yielding with "Yes."
Love is done with and dead; if there lingers
   A faint and indefinite ghost,
It is laid with this kiss on your fingers—
     A jest at the most.

PHILISTIA

'Tis a commonplace, stale situation,
   Now the curtain comes down from above
On the end of our little flirtation —
   A travesty romance; for Love,
If he climbed in disguise to your lattice,
   Fell dead of the first kisses' pain:
But one thing is left us now; that is —
   Begin it again.

GONE

SHE stands upon the steamer's deck;
    The salt wind stings her cheek, goes by,
Comes back with kiss of foamy fleck,
    And sets her jaunty hat awry.

I sit beside the sea-coal glow,
    That with the night wanes less and less:
The room is dark — my heart beats slow
    With silence, loss, and loneliness.

JUST A LOVE-LETTER

"' Miss Blank—at Blank.' Jemima, let it go!"
—*Austin Dobson*

NEW-YORK, July 20, 1883.

DEAR GIRL:
        The town goes on as though
    It thought you still were in it;
The gilded cage seems scarce to know
    That it has lost its linnet;
The people come, the people pass;
    The clock keeps on a-ticking:
And through the basement plots of grass
    Persistent weeds are pricking.

I thought 't would never come—the Spring—
    Since you had left the City:
But on the snow-drifts lingering
    At last the skies took pity,
Then Summer's yellow warmed the sun,
    Daily decreased in distance—
I really don't know how 't was done
    Without your kind assistance.

PHILISTIA

Aunt Van, of course, still holds the fort:
  I've paid the call of duty;
She gave me one small glass of port—
  'Twas '34 and fruity.
The furniture was draped in gloom
  Of linen brown and wrinkled;
I smelt in spots about the room
  The pungent camphor sprinkled.

I sat upon the sofa, where
  You sat and dropped your thimble —
You know — you said you did n't care;
  But I was nobly nimble.
On hands and knees I dropped, and tried
  To — well, I tried to miss it:
You slipped your hand down by your side —
  You knew I meant to kiss it!

Aunt Van, I fear we put to shame
  Propriety and precision:
But, praised be Love, that kiss just came
  Beyond your line of vision.
Dear maiden aunt! the kiss, more sweet
  Because 't is surreptitious,
You never stretched a hand to meet,
  So dimpled, dear, delicious.

PHILISTIA

I sought the Park last Saturday;
   I found the Drive deserted;
The water-trough beside the way
   Sad and superfluous spurted.
I stood where Humboldt guards the gate
   Bronze, bumptious, stained and streaky—
There sat a sparrow on his pate,
   A sparrow chirp and cheeky.

Ten months ago! ten months ago!—
   It seems a happy second,
Against a life-time lone and slow,
   By Love's wild time-piece reckoned—
You smiled, by Aunt's protecting side,
   Where thick the drags were massing,
On one young man who did n't ride,
   But stood and watched you passing.

I haunt Purssell's—to his amaze—
   Not that I care to eat there;
But for the dear clandestine days
   When we two had to meet there.
Oh, blessed is that baker's bake,
   Past cavil and past question;
I ate a bun for your sweet sake,
   And Memory helped Digestion.

PHILISTIA

The Norths are at their Newport ranch;
   Van Brunt has gone to Venice;
Loomis invites me to the Branch,
   And lures me with lawn-tennis.
O bustling barracks by the sea!
   O spiles, canals, and islands!
Your varied charms are naught to me —
   My heart is in the Highlands!

My paper trembles in the breeze
   That all too faintly flutters
Among the dusty city trees,
   And through my half-closed shutters:
A northern captive in the town,
   Its native vigor deadened,
I hope that, as it wandered down,
   Your dear pale cheek it reddened.

I'll write no more. A *vis-à-vis*
   In halcyon vacation
Will sure afford a much more free
   Mode of communication;
I'm tantalized and cribbed and checked
   In making love by letter:
I know a style more brief, direct —
   And generally better!

SHE WAS A BEAUTY

RONDEL

SHE was a beauty in the days
    When Madison was President:
And quite coquettish in her ways—
    On conquests of the heart intent.

Grandpapa, on his right knee bent,
Wooed her in stiff, old-fashioned phrase—
She was a beauty in the days
    When Madison was President.

And when your roses where hers went
Shall go, my Rose, who date from Hayes,
    I hope you'll wear her sweet content
Of whom tradition lightly says:
She was a beauty in the days
    When Madison was President.

CANDOR

OCTOBER—A WOOD

"I KNOW what you 're going to say," she said,
   And she stood up looking uncommonly tall;
"You are going to speak of the hectic Fall,
And say you 're sorry the summer 's dead.
   And no other summer was like it, you know,
   And can I imagine what made it so?
Now are n't you, honestly?" "Yes," I said.

"I know what you 're going to say," she said;
   "You are going to ask if I forget
   That day in June when the woods were wet,
And you carried me"—here she dropped her head—
"Over the creek; you are going to say,
   Do I remember that horrid day.
Now are n't you, honestly?" "Yes," I said.

"I know what you 're going to say," she said;
   "You are going to say that since that time
   You have rather tended to run to rhyme,

And "— her clear glance fell and her cheek grew red —
" And have I noticed your tone was queer?—
   Why, everybody has seen it here!—
Now, are n't you, honestly?"   "Yes," I said.

" I know what you 're going to say," I said;
  " You 're going to say you 've been much annoyed,
    And I 'm short of tact — you will say devoid —
  And I 'm clumsy and awkward, and call me Ted,
    And I bear abuse like a dear old lamb,
    And you 'll have me, anyway, just as I am.
  Now are n't you, honestly?"
                              " Ye-es," she said.

"ACCEPTED"

WE were walking home from meeting, in the calm old country street,
 Where only a glimmer of moonlight through the arch of the elms came down,
And wakened the twinkling shadows that played with her little feet —
 Played hide-and-seek with the little feet that peeped from beneath her gown.

There are things that a girl should n't think, and certainly should n't say —
 But when she says them to *you*, the difference it makes is queer.
And the touch of her hand on my sleeve seemed to ask, in a soft, shy way:
 "Can't you put your arm around me, or is n't it dark enough here?"

A man does n't let that chance slip by him beyond
  recall;
  But I felt that it would n't do, after much con-
  sidering—
Her parents were just ahead, which did n't concern me
  at all—
  But her younger brother behind us—ah, that was a
  different thing!

We reached the dear old homestead the moon made
  tenderly white,
  And stood on the broad front porch, and all of them
  lingered to chat
Of how the soprano had sung and the parson had
  preached that night,
  And how the widow was out in another scandalous
  hat.

A look of appeal from me, and a wonderful glance from
  her,
  And we slipped away from the crowd, unnoticed and
  swift and still—
I think 't was the flower-beds I crossed; but I did n't
  care if it were—
  And she went back through the house, and we met
  at the window-sill.

PHILISTIA

At the window around the corner, with never a soul to see! —
  And I stood on the grass below, and she bent down
    from above,
And the honeysuckles were round us as she stretched
    her arms to me,
  And our lips met there in a new, new kiss — our be-
    trothal gift from Love.

BOHEMIA

A PITCHER OF MIGNONETTE

TRIOLET

A PITCHER of mignonette,
  In a tenement's highest casement:
Queer sort of flower-pot — yet
That pitcher of mignonette
Is a garden in heaven set,
  To the little sick child in the basement —
The pitcher of mignonette,
  In the tenement's highest casement.

POETRY AND THE POET

[A SONNET]

(Found on the Poet's desk)

WEARY, I open wide the antique pane
    I ope to the air
I ope to
I open to the air the antique pane
    And gaze { beyond? / across } the thrift-sown fields of
    wheat, [commonplace?]
    A-shimmering green in breezes born of heat;
And lo!
And high
And my soul's eyes behold { a? / the } billowy main
Whose further shore is Greece   strain
                                                 again
                                                   vain
[Arcadia — mythological allusion.— Mem. : Lemprière.]
    I see thee, Atalanta, vestal fleet,

BOHEMIA

And look! with doves low-fluttering round her feet,
Comes Venus through the golden $\begin{Bmatrix} \text{fields of?} \\ \text{bowing} \end{Bmatrix}$ grain

(Heard by the Poet's neighbor.)

Venus be bothered — it's Virginia Dix!

(Found on the Poet's door.)

Out on important business — back at 6.

YES?

IS it true, then, my girl, that you mean it —
  The word spoken yesterday night?
Does that hour seem so sweet now between it
  And this has come day's sober light?
Have you woke from a moment of rapture
  To remember, regret and repent,
And to hate, perchance, him who has trapped your
  Unthinking consent?

Who was he, last evening — this fellow
  Whose audacity lent him a charm?
Have you promised to wed Pulchinello?
  For life taken Figaro's arm?
Will you have the Court fool of the papers —
  The clown in the journalists' ring,
Who earns his scant bread by his capers,
  To be your heart's king?

BOHEMIA

When we met quite by chance at the theater,
   And I saw you home under the moon,
I 'd no thought, love, that mischief would be at her
   Tricks with my tongue quite so soon;
That I should forget fate and fortune
   Make a difference 'twixt Sèvres and delf—
That I 'd have the calm nerve to impòrtune
   You, sweet, for yourself.

It 's appalling, by Jove, the audacious
   Effrontery of that request!
But you — you grew suddenly gracious,
   And hid your sweet face on my breast.
Why you did it I cannot conjecture:
   I surprised you, poor child, I dare say,
Or perhaps — does the moonlight affect your
   Head often that way

      *   *   *   *

You 're released! With some wooer replace me
   More worthy to be your life's light;
From the tablet of memory efface me,
   If you don't mean your Yes of last night.
But — unless you are anxious to see me a
   Wreck of the pipe and the cup
In my birthplace and grave-yard, Bohemia —
   Love, don't give me up!

A POEM IN THE PROGRAMME

A THOUSAND fans are fretting the hot air;
　　Soft swells the music of the interlude
　Above the murmurous hum of talk subdued;
But from the noise withdrawn and from the glare,
Deep in the shadowy box your coilèd hair
　　Gleams golden-bright, with diamonds bedewed;
　　Your head is bent; I know your dark eyes brood
On the poor sheet of paper you hold there,
That quotes my verses — and I see no more
　　That bald-head Plutus by your side.
　　　　　　　　　　　　　　The seas
　　Sound in my ears; I hear the rustling pines;
Catch the low lisp of billows on the shore
　　Where once I lay in Knickerbockered ease
　　And read to you those then unprinted lines.

BETROTHED

HE SPEAKS

IF when the wild and wintry weather
   Moans baffled round your warm home nest,
And swoops to pluck the light foam-feather
   From off the broad bay's heaving breast;
If then your fancy dim and dreamy
   One careless moment floats to me,
I hope, my sweet, you may not see me
      As others see.

Amid the crowd that glooms and glances—
   A silk sea, islanded with black,
And vexed with local storms of dances —
   I, making slow a sinuous track,
Bow, to the right, to Fan or Florry,
   Nod, to the left, to Nell. And she
Upon my arm, I should be sorry
      You knew knew me.

BOHEMIA

The band above rolls rhythmic thunder
  Down on the whirl and glare below;
The dusty pine-floor pulses under
  The feet that balance to and fro.
Oh! dream of me that ills afflict me;
  Or dream about me not at all;
But do not let your dream depict me
      As at the ball.

With eyes that glisten, hands that tremble:
  With breasts that heave and cheeks that burn,
The gaudy groups disperse, assemble,
  And melt in other groups in turn.
Through flush of paint and frost of powder,
  I see a face or two I've known,
'That, rougeless, donned a carmine prouder
      For me alone.

If this were all, or worst, the whirling
  Among the other fools a fool—
But when I stand my whiskers twirling
  Off by the lobby window cool—
And watch the dance where death's-heads grin to
  Death's-heads, bemasked, beflowered in vain;
See all—and then step reckless into
      That dance again!

BOHEMIA

It were not sin to sin unthinking—
  The drunken sense shall shrive the soul;
But when, withdrawing from the drinking,
  I stand with cursèd self-control—
Ah, then, forgive me then, my pure one!
  Poor, pettier deeds themselves defend;
For time and crime combine to lure one—
    And there's an end.

But, with hard eyes that plead no error,
  To see my Life, sharp-waked from rest—
And then to lull the painted terror
  To smirking slumber on my breast:
To see, beneath the rose and lily,
  The black-rimmed eye, the sallow skin,
As clear as if even now the chilly
    Gray dawn crept in.

Forgive me that!—Who touched my shoulder?
  Oh, it was you, you ivory fan?
Dark domino, with eyes no bolder
  Than should belong, by rights, to Nan.
What's that? Aha, you've caught me moping?
  Fine me a bottle for the wrong—
A quart with silvered shoulders sloping—
    Well, come along!

  *   *   *   *   *   *

BOHEMIA

The whirl has changed to scattered revels,
   The glare to single scattered lights;
A hot and fluctuant draught dishevels
   The hair of Nancy Late-o'-Nights.
Her eyes are largish for their sockets;
   Champagney spray her satin flecks;
And I am feeling in my pockets
   For hat-room checks.

But, you, my fair, unconscious sleeping,
   No dream of day disturbs you yet;
The pale-faced star of love is peeping
   Through morning skies all misty wet.
I leave my partner, flushed and scornful
   Of etiquette, to seek the floor,
I fly, about that hour most mournful
   Of twenty-four.

When dark has lulled the day benighted
   Till dawn reveals the last caress,
And half apart they draw, affrighted
   Each at the other's ghastliness.
When Sleep, with face as blind and ashen
   As Death's, turns restlessly in fear,
As knowing, in some subtle fashion,
   That morn is near.

BOHEMIA

With crisping snow the ground is whitened;
   The horses doze; the hackmen yawn,
Wearily waking; reins are tightened,
   The air is raw with coming dawn.
From the high porch I raise to Venus
   (Whose pallid radiance still endures)
My curse. The hall-door swings between us—
   My sleep and yours.

A thousand miles, a thousand ages
   Our dawns are parted, yours and mine.
For me, by slow and and sickly stages,
   The dull light climbs above the line.
You see, if ever dawn, surprising
   Your slumber, sets your spirit free,
Across white plains a clear sun rising
   Above the sea.

DEAD IN BOHEMIA

IRWIN RUSSELL

DIED IN NEW ORLEANS, DECEMBER, 1879

SMALL was thy share of all this world's delight,
   And scant thy poet's crown of flowers of praise;
  Yet ever catches quaint of quaint old days
Thou sang'st, and, singing, kept thy spirit bright:
Even as to lips the winds of winter bite
   Some outcast wanderer sets his flute and plays
   Till at his feet blossom the icy ways,
And from the snow-drift's bitter wasting white
  He hears the uprising carol of the lark,
   Soaring from clover seas with summer ripe —
    While freeze upon his cheek glad, foolish tears.
  Ah! let us hope that somewhere in thy dark,
   Herrick's full note, and Suckling's pleasant pipe
    Are sounding still their solace in thine ears.

ELSEWHERE

HOLIDAY HOME.

WHEN the Autumn winds nip all the hill-grasses brown,
And sad the last breath of the Summer in town,
When the waves have a chill, with a spicing of salt,
That warms the whole blood like no mortal-brewed malt—
Then I slip the dull burdens of Duty's employ—
New London, New London, New London ahoy!

There the latch-string is out, there's a hand at the door,
There are kindliest faces so kindly before—
Ah, the song takes a lilt, and the words trip with joy,
For New London, New London, New London ahoy!

When the Winter lies white on the roofs of the town,
A sound's in my heart that no storm-wind can drown;
Through the mist and the rain, and the sleet and the snow,
My memory murmurs a melody low,
Like the swing of a song through the brain of a boy—
New London, New London, New London ahoy!

FORFEITS

THEY sent him round the circle fair,
To bow before the prettiest there.
I'm bound to say the choice he made
A creditable taste displayed;
Although — I can't say what it meant —
The little maid looked ill-content.

His task was then anew begun —
To kneel before the wittiest one.
Once more that little maid sought he,
And went him down upon his knee.
She bent her eyes upon the floor —
I think she thought the game a bore.

He circled then — his sweet behest
To kiss the one he loved the best.
For all she frowned, for all she chid,
He kissed that little maid, he did.
And then — though why I can't decide —
The little maid looked satisfied.

IN SCHOOL HOURS

A REAL ROMANCE ?

YOU remember the moments that come
   In a school-day afternoon :
When the illegitimate hum
   Subsides to a drowsy swoon?
When the smell of ink and slates
   Grows oppressively *warm* and thick;
Sleep opens her tempting gates;
   And the clock has a drowsy tick?

Forgetful of watch and rule,
   The teacher has time to think
Of a "recess" in life's long school;
   Of a time to "go out and drink"
At the spring where the Muse has sipped,
   And laurel and bay-leaf bloom —
And a contraband note is slipped,
   Meanwhile, across the room.

ELSEWHERE

From a trembling hand it flies
   Like a little white dove of peace;
And away on its mission it hies
   In an "Atlas of Ancient Greece."
And the sender hides her face;
   For her eyes have a watery shine,
And saline deposits trace
   The recent tear-drop's line.

From the dovecote side it goes
   Across to the ruder half—
Where a large majority shows
   A suppressed desire to laugh.
But the boy that they dare not tease
   Receives the crumpled twist—
And the little hunchback who sees
   Only shakes an impotent fist.

The boy with a fair-curled head
   Smiles with a masculine scorn,
When the sad small note is read,
   With its straggling script forlorn:
"*Charley, wy is it you wont*
   Forgiv me laughfing at you?
I wil kill my self if you dont
   Honest I will for true!"

ELSEWHERE

He responds: He is pleased to find
   She is wiser, at any rate.
He'll be happy to ride behind
   The hearse. May he ask the date?
She reads — with a glittering eye,
   And the look of an angered queen.
This were tragic at thirty. Why
   Is it trivial at thirteen?

Trivial! what shall eclipse
   The pain of our childish woes?
The rose-bud pales its lips
   When a very small zephyr blows.
You smile, O Dian, bland,
   If Endymion's glance is cold:
But Despair seems close at hand
   To that hapless thirteen-year-old.

   *   *   *   *

To the teacher's ears like a dream
   The school-room noises float —
Then a sudden bustle — a scream
   From a girl — "She has cut her throat!"
And the poor little hunchbacked chap
   From his corner leaps like a flash —
Has her death-like head in his lap —
   And his fingers upon the gash.

ELSEWHERE

'T is not deep. An "eraser" blade
   Was the chosen weapon of death;
And the face on the boy's knee laid
   Is alive with a fluttering breath.
But faint from the shock and fright,
   She lies, too weak to be stirred,
Blood-stained, inky and white,
   Pathetic, small, absurd.

The cruel Adonis stands
   Much scared and woe-begone now;
Smoothing with nervous hands
   The damp hair off her brow.
He is penitent, through and through;
   And she — she is satisfied.
Knowing my sex as I do,
   I wish I could add: She died.

THE WAIL OF THE "PERSONALLY CONDUCTED"

CHORUS HEARD ON THE DECK OF A SAGUENAY STEAM-BOAT

INTEGRAL were we, in our old existence ;
Separate beings, individually :
Now are our entities blended, fused and foundered —
We are one person.

We are not mortals, we are not celestials,
We are not birds, the upper ether cleaving,
We are a retrogression toward the monad :
We are Cook's Tourists.

All ways we follow him who holds the guide-book ;
All things we look at, with bedazzled optics ;
Sad are our hearts, because the vulgar rabble
Call us the Cookies.

ELSEWHERE

Happy the man who, by his cheerful fireside,
Says to the partner of his joys and sorrows:
"Anna Maria, let us go to-morrow
    Out for an airing."

Him to Manhattan, or the Beach of Brighton,
Gaily he hieth, or if, fate-accursèd,
Lives he in Boston, still he may betake him
    Daown to Nantasket.

Happy the mortal free and independent,
Master of the mainspring of his own volition!
Look on us with the eye of sweet compassion:
    We are Cook's Tourists.

A CAMPAIGN TORCH

I BLAZED like a meteor through the night
    In the great parade of the great campaign,
A smoke-tailed comet of yellow light
    I wavered and sputtered through wind and rain.
High over the surging crowd I tossed,
    A beacon of battle, flickering free;
And now the contest is gained and lost,
    And victor and victim are one to me.

Ah, never again shall my dinted sides
    Ring responsive when, sharp and clear,
Comes up from the surging human tides
    The rousing sound of the party cheer.
Ah, never again shall my oily blaze
    Blow hither and thither, and fail and flare,
When a thousand masculine marchers raise
    Their "TIGAH!" rending the midnight air.

ELSEWHERE

And never again shall that bright blaze sink,
  When a sudden silence comes over the crowd;
When procession and people, pausing, think,
  And even a heart-beat seems too loud.
When amid the revel of fire and noise
  Comes a thought of the days that were dull and dread,
And through these avenues marched the "Boys"
  Who to-day are heroes — or heroes dead.

When the fingers that hold me grip more slack,
  When the rabble ceases, a space, to rave;
And men's minds travel a score years back,
  And the faces I light grow suddenly grave;
When only the sound of the halting feet
  Like a vanishing rain-fall patters past,
With a muffled fall away down the street,
  And the thundering music stops at last;

When even the buncombe orator, high
  On the flag-draped stand, as he looks around
Finds his breath come short and his throat grow dry,
  While his saw-edged voice has a husky sound;
Feeling, for once in his life, afraid;
  Remembering — ay, he remembered then!
That statecraft is not a tricky trade,
  That he deals with the honor and hopes of men.

ELSEWHERE

No more my spirit of flame shall thrill
    As then: no more shall it leap and play
When the moment's madness masters the will,
    And the roaring column marches away.

   *   *   *   *   *

No more! By November's night-winds fanned,
    In the gusty lee of a Bowery porch,
You may see me lighting a pea-nut stand —
    The battered wreck of a Campaign Torch.

November, 1880.

HOME, SWEET HOME, WITH VARIATIONS

Being Suggestions of the Various Styles in which an Old Theme might have been Treated by Certain Metrical Composers

FANTASIA

I

The Original Theme, as John Howard Payne Wrote it:

'MID pleasures and palaces though we may roam,
    Be it ever so humble, there's no place like home!
A charm from the skies seems to hallow us there,
Which, seek through the world, is not met with elsewhere.

    Home, Home! Sweet, Sweet Home!
    There's no place like Home!

ELSEWHERE

An exile from home, splendor dazzles in vain!
Oh, give me my lowly thatched cottage again!
The birds singing gayly that came at my call!
Give me them! and the peace of mind dearer than all.

Home, Home! Sweet, Sweet Home!
There's no place like Home!

II

As Algernon Charles Swinburne might have Wrapped it up in Variations:

['*Mid pleasures and palaces—*]

AS sea-foam blown of the winds, as blossom of brine that is drifted
Hither and yon on the barren breast of the breeze,
Though we wander on gusts of a god's breath shaken and shifted,
The salt of us stings and is sore for the sobbing seas.
For home's sake hungry at heart, we sicken in pillared porches.
Of bliss made sick for a life that is barren of bliss,
For the place whereon is a light out of heaven that sears not nor scorches,
Nor elsewhere than this.

ELSEWHERE

[*An exile from home, splendor dazzles in vain—*]

For here we know shall no gold thing glisten,
  No bright thing burn, and no sweet thing shine;
Nor Love lower never an ear to listen
  To words that work in the heart like wine.
    What time we are set from our land apart,
    For pain of passion and hunger of heart,
Though we walk with exiles fame faints to christen,
  Or sing at the Cytherean's shrine.

[VARIATION: *An exile from home—*]

    Whether with him whose head
    Of gods is honorèd,
With song made splendent in the sight of men—
    Whose heart most sweetly stout,
    From ravished France cast out,
Being firstly hers, was hers most wholly then—
    Or where on shining seas like wine
  The dove's wings draw the drooping Erycine.

[*Give me my lowly thatched cottage—*]

    For Joy finds Love grow bitter,
    And spreads his wings to quit her,
    At thought of birds that twitter
      Beneath the roof-tree's straw—

ELSEWHERE

Of birds that come for calling,
No fear or fright appalling,
When dews of dusk are falling,
Or daylight's draperies draw.

[*Give me them, and the peace of mind* —]

Give me these things then back, though the giving
   Be at cost of earth's garner of gold;
There is no life without these worth living,
   No treasure where these are not told.
For the heart give the hope that it knows not,
   Give the balm for the burn of the breast —
For the soul and the mind that repose not,
   O, give us a rest!

III

As Mr. Francis Bret Harte might have Woven it into a Touching Tale of a Western Gentleman in a Red Shirt:

BROWN o' San Juan,
   Stranger, I'm Brown.
Come up this mornin' from 'Frisco —
   Be'n a-saltin' my specie-stacks down.

ELSEWHERE

Be'n a-knockin' around,
   Fer a man from San Juan,
Putty consid'able frequent —
   Jes' catch onter that streak o' the dawn !

Right thar lies my home —
   Right thar in the red —
I could slop over, stranger, in po'try
   Would spread out old Shakspoke cold dead.

Stranger, you freeze to this: there ain't no kinder gin-palace,
Nor no variety-show lays over a man's own rancho.
Maybe it hain't no style, but the Queen in the Tower o' London
Ain't got naathin' I'd swop for that house over thar on the hill-side.

Thar is my ole gal, 'n' the kids, 'n' the rest o' my live-stock ;
Thar my Remington hangs, and thar there's a griddle-cake br'ilin' —
For the two of us, pard — and thar, I allow, the heavens
Smile more friendly-like than on any other locality.

ELSEWHERE

Stranger, nowhere else I don't take no satisfaction.
Gimme my ranch, 'n' them friendly old Shanghai
    chickens —
I brung the original pair f'm the States in eighteen-'n'-
    fifty —
Gimme them and the feelin' of solid domestic comfort.

    Yer parding, young man —
        But this landscape a kind
    Er flickers — I 'low 'twuz the po'try —
        I thought thet my eyes hed gone blind.

*   *   *   *   *

    Take that pop from my belt!
        Hi, thar! — gimme yer han' —
    Or I 'll kill myself — Lizzie! — she 's left me —
        Gone off with a purtier man!

    Thar, I 'll quit — the ole gal
        An' the kids — run away!
    I be derned! Howsomever, come in, pard —
        The griddle-cake 's thar, anyway.

ELSEWHERE

IV

AS AUSTIN DOBSON MIGHT HAVE TRANSLATED IT FROM HORACE, IF IT HAD EVER OCCURRED TO HORACE TO WRITE IT:

RONDEAU

> Palatiis in remotis voluptates
> Si quæris . . .
> — FLACCUS, Q. HORATIUS, *Carmina*, *Lib. V: 1.*

AT home alone, O Nomades,
   Although Mæcenas' marble frieze
  Stand not between you and the sky,
  Nor Persian luxury supply
Its rosy surfeit, find ye ease.

Tempt not the far Ægean breeze;
With home-made wine and books that please,
  To duns and bores the door deny
        At home, alone.

Strange joys may lure. Your deities
Smile here alone. Oh, give me these:
  Low eaves, where birds familiar fly,
  And peace of mind, and, fluttering by,
My Lydia's graceful draperies,
        At home, *alone*.

ELSEWHERE

V

AS IT MIGHT HAVE BEEN CONSTRUCTED IN 1744,
OLIVER GOLDSMITH, AT 19, WRITING THE
FIRST STANZA, AND ALEXANDER POPE,
AT 52, THE SECOND:

HOME! at the word, what blissful visions rise;
Lift us from earth, and draw toward the skies:
'Mid mirag'd towers, or meretricious joys,
Although we roam, one thought the mind employs:
Or lowly hut, good friend, or loftiest dome,
Earth knows no spot so holy as our Home.
There, where affection warms the father's breast,
There is the spot of heav'n most surely blest.
Howe'er we search, though wandering with the wind
Through frigid Zembla, or the heats of Ind,
Not elsewhere may we seek, nor elsewhere know,
The light of heav'n upon our dark below.

When from our dearest hope and haven reft,
Delight nor dazzles, nor is luxury left,
We long, obedient to our nature's law,
To see again our hovel thatched with straw:
See birds that know our avenaceous store
Stoop to our hand, and thence repleted soar:
But, of all hopes the wanderer's soul that share,
His pristine peace of mind's his final prayer.

ELSEWHERE

VI

As Walt Whitman might have Written all around it:

I

YOU over there, young man with the guide-book, red-bound, covered flexibly with red linen,
Come here, I want to talk with you; I, Walt, the Manhattanese, citizen of these States, call you.
Yes, and the courier, too, smirking, smug-mouthed, with oil'd hair; a garlicky look about him generally; him, too, I take in, just as I would a coyote, or a king, or a toad-stool, or a ham-sandwich, or anything or anybody else in the world.
Where are you going?
You want to see Paris, to eat truffles, to have a good time; in Vienna, London, Florence, Monaco, to have a good time; you want to see Venice.
Come with me. I will give you a good time; I will give you all the Venice you want, and most of the Paris.
I, Walt, I call to you. I am all on deck! Come and loafe with me! Let me tote you around by your elbow and show you things.
You listen to my ophicleide!
Home!

ELSEWHERE

Home, I celebrate. I elevate my fog-whistle, inspir'd by the thought of home.

Come in! — take a front seat; the jostle of the crowd not minding; there is room enough for all of you.

This is my exhibition — it is the greatest show on earth — there is no charge for admission.

All you have to pay me is to take in my romanza.

2

1. The brown-stone house; the father coming home worried from a bad day's business; the wife meets him in the marble-pav'd vestibule; she throws her arms about him; she presses him close to her; she looks him full in the face with affectionate eyes; the frown from his brow disappearing.

Darling, she says, *Johnny has fallen down and cut his head; the cook is going away, and the boiler leaks.*

2. The mechanic's dark little third-story room, seen in a flash from the Elevated Railway train; the sewing-machine in a corner; the small cook-stove; the whole family eating cabbage around a kerosene lamp; of the clatter and roar and groaning wail of the Elevated train unconscious; of the smell of the cabbage unconscious.

me, passant, in the train, of the cabbage not quite so unconscious.

3. The French flat; the small rooms, all right-angles, unindividual; the narrow halls; the gaudy cheap decorations everywhere.

The janitor and the cook exchanging compliments up and down the elevator-shaft; the refusal to send up more coal, the solid splash of the water upon his head, the language he sends up the shaft, the triumphant laughter of the cook, to her kitchen retiring.

4. The widow's small house in the suburbs of the city; the widow's boy coming home from his first day down town; he is flushed with happiness and pride; he is no longer a school-boy, he is earning money; he takes on the airs of a man and talks learnedly of business.

5. The room in the third-class boarding-house; the mean little hard-coal fire, the slovenly Irish servant-girl making it, the ashes on the hearth, the faded furniture, the private provender hid away in the closet, the dreary back-yard out the window; the young girl at the glass, with her mouth full of hair-pins, doing up her hair to go down-stairs and flirt with the young fellows in the parlor.

6. The kitchen of the old farm-house; the young convict just return'd from prison — it was his first offense, and the judges were lenient to him.

ELSEWHERE

He is taking his first meal out of prison; he has been receiv'd back, kiss'd, encourag'd to start again; his lungs, his nostrils expand with the big breaths of free air; with shame, with wonderment, with a trembling joy, his heart too expanding.

The old mother busies herself about the table; she has ready for him the dishes he us'd to like; the father sits with his back to them, reading the newspaper, the newspaper shaking and rustling much; the children hang wondering around the prodigal — they have been caution'd: *Do not ask where our Jim has been; only say you are glad to see him.*

The elder daughter is there, pale-fac'd, quiet; her young man went back on her four years ago; his folks would not let him marry a convict's sister. She sits by the window, sewing on the children's clothes, the clothes not only patching up; her hunger for children of her own invisibly patching up.

The brother looks up; he catches her eye, he fearful, apologetic; she smiles back at him, not reproachfully smiling, with loving pretense of hope smiling — it is too much for him; he buries his face in the folds of the mother's black gown.

7. The best room of the house, on the Sabbath only open'd; the smell of horse-hair furniture and mahogany varnish; the ornaments on the what-not in the

ELSEWHERE

corner; the wax fruit, dusty, sunken, sagged in, consumptive-looking, under a glass globe; the sealing-wax imitation of coral; the cigar boxes with shells plastered over; the perforated card-board motto.

The kitchen; the housewife sprinkling the clothes for the fine ironing to-morrow — it is Third-day night, and the plain things are already iron'd, now in cupboards, in drawers stowed away.

The wife waiting for the husband — he is at the tavern, jovial, carousing; she, alone in the kitchen sprinkling clothes — the little red wood clock with peaked top, with pendulum wagging behind a pane of gayly painted glass, strikes twelve.

The sound of the husband's voice on the still night air — he is singing: *We won't go home till morning!* — the wife arising, toward the wood-shed hastily going, stealthily entering, the voice all the time coming nearer, inebriate, chantant.

The wood-shed; the club behind the door of the wood-shed; the wife annexing the club; the husband approaching, always inebriate, chantant.

The husband passing the door of the wood-shed; the club over his head, now with his head in contact; the sudden cessation of the song; the temperance pledge signed the next morning; the benediction of peace over the domestic foyer temporarily resting.

ELSEWHERE

3

I sing the soothing influences of home.
You, young man, thoughtlessly wandering, with courier, with guide-book wandering,
You hearken to the melody of my steam-calliope.
Yawp!

ULTIMA THULE

FORTY

IN the heyday of my years, when I thought the world was young,
    And believed that I was old — at the very gates of Life —
It seemed in every song the birds of heaven sung
    That I heard the sweet injunction: "Go get thee a wife!"

And within the breast of youth woke a secret sweet desire;
    For Love spoke in that carol his first mysterious word,
That to-day through ashen years kindles memory into fire,
    Though the birds are dead that sang it, and the heart is old that heard.

I have watched my youth's blue heavens flush to angry, brooding red,
    And again the crimson palsied in a dull, unpregnant gloom;
I am older than some sorrows; I have watched by Pleasure dead;
    I have seen Hope grow immortal at the threshold of the tomb.

ULTIMA THULE

Through the years by turns that gave me now curses, now caresses,
  I have fought a fight with Fortune wherein Love hath had no part;
To-day, when peace hard-conquered ripe years and weary blesses,
  Will my fortieth summer pardon twenty winters to my heart?

When the spring-tide verdure darkens to the summer's deeper glories,
  And in the thickening foliage doth the year its life renew,
Will to me the forests whisper once more their wind-learnt stories?
  Will the birds their message bring me from out the heaven of blue?

Will the wakened world sing for me the old enchanted song —
  Touch the underflow of love that, through all the toil and strife,
Has only grown the stronger as the years passed lone and long?
  Shall I learn the will of Heaven is to get me a wife?

ULTIMA THULE

The boy's heart yearns for freedom, he walks hand-in-hand with pleasure;
Made bright with wine and kisses, he sees the face of Life;
He would make the world a pleasaunce for a love that knows not measure;
But the man secks Heaven, and finds it in the bosom of his wife.

STRONG AS DEATH

O DEATH, when thou shalt come to me
From out thy dark, where she is now,
Come not with graveyard smell on thee,
  Or withered roses on thy brow.

Come not, O Death, with hollow tone,
  And soundless step, and clammy hand—
Lo, I am now no less alone
  Than in thy desolate, doubtful land;

But with that sweet and subtle scent
  That ever clung about her (such
As with all things she brushed was blent);
  And with her quick and tender touch.

ULTIMA THULE

With the dim gold that lit her hair,
   Crown thyself, Death; let fall thy tread
So light that I may dream her there,
   And turn upon my dying bed.

And through my chilling veins shall flame
   My love, as though beneath her breath;
And in her voice but call my name,
   And I will follow thee, O Death.

DEAF

AS to a bird's song she were listening,
　　Her beautiful head is ever sidewise bent;
　Her questioning eyes lift up their depths intent —
She, who will never hear the wild-birds sing.
My words within her ears' cold chambers ring
　　Faint, with the city's murmurous sub-tones blent;
　　Though with such sounds as suppliants may have sent
To high-throned goddesses, my speech takes wing.

Not for the side-poised head's appealing grace
　　I gaze, nor hair where fire in shadow lies —
For her this world's unhallowed noises base
　　Melt into silence; not our groans, our cries,
Our curses, reach that high-removèd place
　　Where dwells her spirit, innocently wise.

LES MORTS VONT VITE

LES morts vont vite! Ay, for a little space
We miss and mourn them, fallen from their place;
To take our portion in their rest are fain;
But by-and-by, having wept, press on again,
Perchance to win their laurels in the race.

What man would find the old in the new love's face?
Seek on the fresher lips the old kisses' trace?
For withered roses newer blooms disdain?
Les morts vont vite!

But when disease brings thee in piteous case,
Thou shalt thy dead recall, and thy ill grace
To them for whom remembrance plead in vain.
Then, shuddering, think, while thy bed-fellow Pain
Clasps thee with arms that cling like Death's embrace:
Les morts vont vite!

DISASTER

A ROAR of voices and a tottering town,
A dusty ruin of high walls crumbling down,

A wild, blind hurrying of men mad with fear,
Rushing from death to death — above, the clear,

Calm, pitiless, lurid orange of the sky,
Where one affrighted vulture dares to fly.

On either side an ocean's overflow;
And fume and thunder of hid fires below.

* * *

Then, when the next morn breaks, fair, heartless, bland,
The young west wind strews a dead world with sand:

Follows the broad and jagged swath where Fate
Has mown a thousand corpses mutilate.

ULTIMA THULE

And on the writhen faces bends to see
Unspeakable fear, defiance, agony.

Sees life's vain protest turned to impotent stone,
Dumbly reproachful still, and sees, alone,

Smiling in death, serene, sweet, undistressed,
One woman with a cancer at her breast.

SEPTEMBER

RONDEAU

THE Summer's gone — how did it go?
And where has gone the dogwood's snow?
    The air is sharp upon the hill,
    And with a tinkle sharp and chill
The icy little brooklets flow.

What is it in the season, though,
Brings back the days of old, and so
    Sets memory recalling still
        The Summers gone?

Why are my days so dark? for lo!
The maples with fresh glory glow,
    Fair shimmering mists the valleys fill,
    The keen air sets the blood a-thrill —
Ah! now that *you* are gone, I know
        The Summer's gone.

THEN

WHEN, moved by sudden strange desires,
    And innocent shames and sweet distress,
Your eyes grow large and moist, your lips
Pout to a kiss, while virgin fires
    Run flushing to your finger tips—
Then I will tell you what you guess.

THE APPEAL TO HAROLD [3]

HARO! Haro!
    Judge now betwixt this woman and me,
    Haro!
She leaves me bond, who found me free.
Of love and hope she hath drained me dry—
Yea, barren as a drought-struck sky;
She hath not left me tears for weeping,
Nor will my eyelids close in sleeping.
I have gathered all my life's-blood up—
    Haro!
She hath drunk and thrown aside the cup.

ULTIMA THULE

Shall she not give me back my days?
      Haro!
I made them perfect for her praise.
There was no flower in all the brake
I found not fairer for her sake;
There was no sweet thought I did not fashion
For aid and servant to my passion.
Labor and learning worthless were,
      Haro!
Save that I made them gifts for her.

Shall she not give me back my nights?
      Haro!
Give me sweet sleep for brief delights?
Lo, in the night's wan mid I lie,
And ghosts of hours that are dead go by:
Hours of a love that died unshriven;
Of a love in change for my manhood given:
She caressed and slew my soul's white truth,
      Haro!
Shall she not give me back my youth?

Haro! Haro!
Tell thou me not of a greater judge,
      Haro!
It is He who hath my sin in grudge.
Yea, from God I appeal to thee;

ULTIMA THULE

God hath not part or place for me.
Thou who hast sinned, judge thou my sinning:
I have staked my life for a woman's winning;
She hath stripped me of all save remembering—
      Haro!
Right thou me, right thou me, Harold the King!

TO A DEAD WOMAN

NOT a kiss in life; but one kiss, at life's end,
I have set on the face of Death in trust for thee.
Through long years keep it fresh on thy lips, O friend!
At the gate of Silence give it back to me.

THE OLD FLAG

OFF with your hat as the flag goes by!
   And let the heart have its say;
You 're man enough for a tear in your eye
   That you will not wipe away.

You 're man enough for a thrill that goes
   To your very finger-tips —
Ay! the lump just then in your throat that rose
   Spoke more than your parted lips.

Lift up the boy on your shoulder, high,
   And show him the faded shred —
Those stripes would be red as the sunset sky
   If Death could have dyed them red.

The man that bore it with Death has lain
   This twenty years and more;—
He died that the work should not be vain
   Of the men who bore it before.

ULTIMA THULE

The man that bears it is bent and old,
    And ragged his beard and gray,—
But look at his eye fire young and bold,
    At the tune that he hears them play.

The old tune thunders through all the air,
    And strikes right in to the heart;—
If ever it calls for *you*, boy, be there!
    Be there, and ready to start.

Off with your hat as the flag goes by!
    Uncover the youngster's head!
Teach him to hold it holy and high,
    For the sake of its sacred dead.

Evacuation Day, 1883.

FROM A COUNTING-HOUSE

THERE is an hour when first the westering sun
    Takes on some forecast faint of future red;
When from the wings of weariness is shed
A spell upon us toilers, every one;
The day's work lags a little, well-nigh done;
    Far dusky lofts through all the close air spread
    A smell of eastern bales; the old clerk's head
Nods by my side, heavy with dreams begun
In dear dead days wherein his heart is tombed.
    But I my way to Italy have found;
        Or wander where high stars gleam coldly through
The Alpine skies; or in some nest perfumed,
    With soft Parisian luxury set round,
        Hold out my arms and cry " At last! " to you.

TO A HYACINTH PLUCKED FOR DECORATION DAY

O FLOWER, plucked before the dew
Could wet thy thirsty petals blue—
Grieve not! a dearer dew for thee
Shall be the tears of Memory.

LONGFELLOW

POET whose sunny span of fruitful years
    Outreaches earth, whose voice within our ears
Grows silent — shall we mourn for thee? Our sigh
    Is April's breath, our grief is April's tears.

If this be dying, fair it is to die.
    Even as a garment weariness lays by,
Thou layest down life to pass, as Time hath passed,
    From wintry rigors to a Springtime sky.

Are there tears left to give thee at the last,
    Poet of spirits crushed and hearts down-cast,
Loved of worn women who, when work is done,
    Weep o'er thy page in twilights fading fast?

ULTIMA THULE

Oh, tender-toned and tender-hearted one,
  We give thee to the season new begun —
Lay thy white head within the arms of Spring —
  Thy song had all her shower and her sun.

Nay, let us not such sorrowful tribute bring,
  Now that thy lark-like soul hath taken wing:
A grateful memory fills and more endears
  The silence when a bird hath ceased to sing.

FOR THE FIRST PAGE OF THE ALBUM

I OPEN this to write for her
   Within whose gates is ever Peace;
Beneath whose roof the wanderer
   Finds from his wayside cares release.

Her presence is in every room,
   Her silent love is everywhere,
As pleasant as a soft perfume,
   As soothing as a twilight air.

No song shall tell the friendly debt
   My gratitude were glad to pay;
But here may other singers set
   The half of what I fain would say.

More sweetly may their songs be made,
   Their lines in purer cadence fall,
Yet none — yet none leaves more unsaid,
   With truer wish to say it all.

September 10. 1883.

FAREWELL TO SALVINI [4]

April 26th, 1883

ALTHOUGH a curtain of the salt sea-mist
   May fall between the actor and our eyes—
   Although he change for dear and softer skies
These that the sun has yet but coyly kissed—
Although the voice to which we loved to list
   Fail ere the thunder of our plaudits dies—
   Although he parts from us in gracious wise,
With grateful memory left his eulogist—
   His best is with us still.
                             His perfect art
Has held us 'twixt a heart-throb and a tear—
   Cheating our souls to passionate belief.
And in his greatness we have now some part—
   We have been courtiers of the crownless Lear,
   And partners in Othello's mighty grief.

ON READING A POET'S FIRST BOOK

THIS is a breath of summer wind
   That comes — we know not how — that goes
As softly, — leaving us behind
   Pleased with a smell of vine and rose.

Poet, shall this be all thy word?
   Blow on us with a bolder breeze;
Until we rise, as having heard
   The sob, the song of far-off seas.

Blow in thy shell until thou draw,
   From inner whorls where still they sleep,
The notes unguessed of love and awe,
   And all thy song grow full and deep.

ULTIMA THULE

Feeble may be the scanty phrase —
    Thy dream a dream tongue never spake —
Yet shall thy note, through doubtful days,
    Swell stronger for Endeavor's sake.

As Jacob, wrestling through the night,
    Felt all his muscles strengthen fast
With wakening strength, and met the light
    Blessèd and strong, though overcast.

FEMININE

SHE might have known it in the earlier Spring,
  That all my heart with vague desire was stirred;
And, ere the Summer winds had taken wing,
  I told her; but she smiled and said no word.

The Autumn's eager hand his red gold grasped,
  And she was silent; till from skies grown drear
Fell soft one fine, first snow-flake, and she clasped
  My neck and cried, "Love, we have lost a year!"

REDEMPTION

AS to the drunkard who · at morn doth wake
    Are the clear waters of the virgin spring
Wherewith he bathes his eyes that burn and sting
And his intolerable thirst doth slake,
So is the thought of thee to me, who break
    One sober moment, sick and shuddering,
    From all my life's unworthiness, to fling
Me at thy memory's feet, and for Love's sake
Pray that thy peace may enter in my soul.
    Love, thou hast heard! My veins more calmly flow—
    The madness of the night is passed away—
Fire of false eyes, thirst of the cursèd bowl—
    I drink deep of thy purity, and lo!
    Thou hast given me new heart to meet the day.

TRIUMPH

THE dawn came in through the bars of the blind,—
And the winter's dawn is gray,—
And said—However you cheat your mind,
　The hours are flying away.

A ghost of a dawn, and pale and weak—
　Has the sun a heart, I said,
To throw a morning flush on the cheek
　Whence a fairer flush has fled?

As a gray rose-leaf that is fading white
　Was the cheek where I set my kiss;
And on that side of the bed all night
　Death had watched, and I on this.

I kissed her lips, they were half apart,
　Yet they made no answering sign;
Death's hand was on her failing heart,
　And his eyes said—"She is mine."

ULTIMA THULE

I set my lips on the blue-veined lid,
  Half-veiled by her death-damp hair;
And oh, for the violet depths it hid,
  And the light I longed for there!

Faint day and the fainter life awoke,
  And the night was overpast;
And I said — " Though never in life you spoke,
  Oh, speak with a look at last ! "

For the space of a heart-beat fluttered her breath,
  As a bird's wing spread to flee;
She turned her weary arms to Death,
  And the light of her eyes to me.

TO HER

Perchance the spell that now must part
    Our lives may yet be broken;
And then your sweet unconscious heart
    May know my love unspoken.
Perchance the jealous seal of Time
    May break in some far season;
And you will read this book of rhyme,
    And know the rhyme's dear reason.

How long ago the song began!
    How lonely was the singer,
Whose mistress never thought to scan
    The lines he dared to bring her!
Oh, will you ever read it true,
    When all the rhymes are ended—
How much of Hope, of Love, of You,
    With every verse was blended.

Who knows? But when the bars shall fall
    That set our souls asunder,
May you, at last, in hearing all,
    Feel Love grow out of Wonder;
And may the song be glad as when
    The boy's fresh voice commenced it;
And may my heart be beating then,
    To feel your own against it!

ROWEN
"SECOND CROP" SONGS
[1892]

TO A. L. B.

I put your rose within our baby's hand,
To bear back with him into Baby-land;
Your rose, you grew it — O my ever dear,
What roses you have grown me, year by year!
Your lover finds no path too hard to go
While your love's roses round about him blow.

October, 1892.

*WHY do I love New York, my dear?
I know not. Were my father here—
And his —— and HIS —— the three and I
Might, perhaps, make you some reply.*

AT THE CENTENNIAL BALL—1889

AN OLD MAN'S OLD FANCIES

THERE 'S the music—go, my sweet,
    I will sit and watch you here;
There 's a tingling in my feet
    I 've not felt this many a year.
    But my music 's done, my dear—
'T is enough this heart can beat
    Time to strains that stir your heart;
'T is enough these eyes can see
    Fresh young fires of pleasure start
In the eyes you turn to me.
    Loving, yet, my dear,
    Loath to linger here —
Music-maddened, all impatient to be free.

ROWEN

Go, the music swells and rises — go!
    Younger faces wait you where
    All a-tremble is the air,
And a rhythmic murmur low
    Wavers to and fro —
Life and dance and clasp of lover's hands await you there.
Go, my child, with cheeks that burn,
    Eyes that shine, and fluttering breast,
Go, and leave me — not alone!
    In the dance you shall be prest
Close, and all your soul shall turn
    Tender at the music's tone;
        But more close, more tenderly
        Shall the exultant harmony
Speak to this old, awakened heart, that hears
    The voices of dead years.

She goes — and from below, up-springing,
    The stress and swell of lilting sound
Set one vast field of color swinging
    In sinuous measure round and round.
        The fiddle-bows go up in the air,
            And the fiddle-bows go down;
        And the girl of mine with the yellow hair
        Is dancing to an old-time air
            With the maids of New York town.

ROWEN

My eyes grow dim to see;
But the music sends a song to me,
And here 's the song that comes from below —
From the dancing tip of the fiddle-bow:

THE BALL—1789

THE Town is at the Ball to-night,
    The Town is at the Ball;
From the Battery to Hickory Lane
    The Beaux come one and all.
The French folk up along the Sound
    Took carriage for the city,
And Madge the Belle, from New Rochelle,
    Will stop with Lady Kitty.

And if the Beaux could have their way
    Their choice would be, in Brief,
That Madge the Belle should lead the ball
    And open with THE CHIEF.
Though Lady Kitty's high estate
    May give his choice some reason,
By Right Divine Madge holds her place —
    The Toast of all the Season.

ROWEN

Behold her as she trips the floor
  By Lady Kitty's side —
How low bows Merit at her glance,
  And Valor, true and tried!
Each hand that late the sword-hilt grasped
  Would fain her hand be pressing —
But, ah! fair Madge, who 'll wear your badge
  Is past all wooer's guessing.

The Colonel bows his powdered head
  Well nigh unto her feet;
Fame's Trump rings dull unto his ears,
  That wait her Accents sweet.
The young Leftenant, Trig and Trim,
  Who lately won his spurs,
Casts love-sick glances in her way,
  And wins no glance of hers.

Before her bows the Admiral,
  Whose head was never bowed
Before the foamy-crested wave
  That wet the straining shroud.
And all his pretty midshipmen,
  They stand there in a line,
Saluting this Fair Craft that sails
  With no surrendering sign.

ROWEN

And so she trips across the floor
  On Lady Kitty's arm,
And grizzled pates and frizzled pates
  All bow before her charm.
And she will dance the minuet,
  A-facing Lady Kitty,
Nor miss THE CHIEF—she hath, in brief,
  Her choice of all the city.

*　　*　　*　　*　　*　　*

But in the minuet a hand
  Shall touch her finger-tips,
And almost to a Kiss shall turn
  The Smile upon her lips;
And he is but a midship boy,
  And she is Madge the Belle;
But never to Chief nor to Admiral
  Such a tale her lips shall tell.

*　　*　　*　　*　　*　　*

The Town is at the Ball to-night,
  The Town is at the Ball,
And the Town shall talk as never before
  Ere another night shall fall;
And men shall rave in Rector street,
  And men shall swear in Pine,
And hearts shall break for Madge's sake
  From Bay to City Line.

ROWEN

And Lady Kit shall wring her hands,
  And write the tale to tell
(To that much dreaded Maiden Aunt
  Who lives at New Rochelle)
All of a gallant Midshipman
  Who wooed in April weather
The Fairest of All at the Chieftain's Ball—
  And they ran away together!

And from below the music flowing
  Has taken a measured, mocking fall,
And forward, backward, coming, going,
  They dance the Minuet of the Ball.
And even as once her grandmama
  Went flitting to and fro
In a dance she danced with grandpapa
  One hundred years ago—
    So, while the fiddle-bows go up,
      And the fiddle-bows go down,
    A daughter of mine with yellow hair
    Is dancing to an old-time air
      With the maids of New York town.

And now again, in cadence changing,
  The music takes a waltzing swing,
And sets an old man's fancies ranging
  Among the tunes his memories sing:—

ROWEN

I hear a sound of strings long slackened,
  The hum of many a stringless bow
On fiddles broken, warped and blackened
  With dust of years of long ago;
And hear the waltz that thrilled and quivered
  Along the yearning pulse of youth,
And unto two dumb hearts delivered
  The message of Love's hidden truth.

THE BALL — 1861

TO the front at morn!
To the front at the break of day!
And the transport ship lies tossing on the waves of the lower bay.

Her sails are white
In the silver stream of the moon;
The moon will soon be red as blood, her sails will be reddened soon.

To us who go
Is given a dance to-night —
We may clasp our arms around women and gather the strength to fight.

ROWEN

Clasp Heaven so close!
Look in Love's eyes and part!
Will the bullet that kills the body make an end of the hunger of heart?

To our breasts they strain,
Beautiful, warm with life—
Make men of us who would make us heroes for mortal strife.

Can I hold you thus,
And release you, all unsaid?
Know I shall want you, dead or living, and dream you may want me, dead?

The last, last dance—
For the gray of the morn is near—
Cling to me once, till I learn the tune that shall outsing Death at my ear!

Cling to me once, but once—
This is my whole life's round!
Give me to face Death's silence this moment of motion and sound.

* * * * * *

ROWEN

Then, as the word unsaid
Found voice in the music's tone,
She looked in my face, and I knew that my soul should
    not go alone.

And the gray dawn came,
But to us had come a light
To make the face of Life and the face of Death shine
    bright.

* * * * * *

To the front at morn!
To the front at the break of day!
Farewell, I said, my Love, and love went with me upon
    my way.

So, through the weary years
Of prayers and tears
　　She waited for me, till I came at last;
Came when the soldier's work was done,
And the one holy end of war was won,
　　And parting-time was past.

And once again the old tune, winging
　　Its way to hearts that still were young,
Set brain and pulse and spirit swinging,
　　And once again to me she clung.

ROWEN

And then — but, ah! my music's done —
  For this short way I have to go
An old tune in my mind may run
  That she and I once used to know,
And make an old man's memories stir —
  But all earth's music died with her.
But for you below, my sweet —
  You she left me — still for you
Bowstrings quiver, batons beat,
 . And the fiddles thrill you through.
Yours it is to dance, and still,
  Dancing, you may look in eyes
Quick to love you, if you will —
  Quick to turn to high emprise
When the land that gave them birth
Makes the test of manhood's worth.

But, for me, my music's done, —
  I can only sit and hear
Through your whirl of tunes the one
  That Love holds dear.

While the fiddle-bows go up in the air,
  And the fiddle-bows go down,
And the girl of mine with the yellow hair
Is dancing to an old-time air
  With the maids of New York town.

THERE'S but one thing to sing about,
 And poor's the song that does without;
And many a song would not live long
Were it not for the theme that is never worked out.

THE LAST OF THE NEW YEAR'S CALLERS

THE STORY OF AN OLD MAN, AN OLD MAN'S FRIENDSHIP, AND A NEW CARD-BASKET

THE door is shut — I think the fine old face
   Trembles a little, round the under lip;
His look is wistful — can it be the place
   Where, at his knock, the bolt was quick to slip
(It had a knocker then), when, bravely decked,
   He took, of New Year's, with his lowest bow,
His glass of egg-nog, white and nutmeg-flecked,
   From her who is — where is the young bride now?

O Greenwood, answer! Through your ample gate
   There went a hearse, these many years ago;
And often by a grave — more oft of late —
   Stands an old gentleman, with hair like snow.
Two graves he stands by, truly; for the friend
   Who won her, long has lain beside his wife;
And their old comrade, waiting for the end,
   Remembers what they were to him in life.

ROWEN

And now he stands before the old-time door,
  A little gladdened in his lonely heart
To give of love for those that are no more
  To those that live to-day a generous part.
Ay, *She* has gone, sweet, loyal, brave and gay —
  But then, her daughter's grown and wed the while;
And the old custom lingers: New Year's Day,
  Will not she greet him with her mother's smile?

But things are changed, ah, changed, you see;
We keep no New Year's, now, not we —
    It's an old-time day,
    And an old-time way,
And an old-time fashion we've chosen to cut —
    And the dear old man
    May wait as he can
In front of the old-time door that's *shut.*

MAY-BLOOM

OH, for you that I never knew! —
    Now that the Spring is swelling,
And over the way is a whitening may,
    In the yard of my neighbor's dwelling.

O may, oho! Do your sisters blow
    Out there in the country grasses,
A-mocking the white of the cloudlet light
    That up in the blue sky passes?

Here in town the grass it is brown
    Right under your beautiful clusters;
But your sisters thrive where the sward 's alive
    With emerald lights and lusters.

Dream of my dreams! vision that seems
    Ever to scorn my praying,
Love that I wait, face of my fate,
    Come with me now a-maying.

ROWEN

Soul of my soul! all my life long,
      Looking for you I wander;
Long have I sought — shall I find naught
      Under the may-bushes yonder?

Oh, for you that I never knew,
      Only in dreams that bind you! —
By Spring's own grace I shall know your face
      When under the may I find you!

THE LINNET

ALL day he sat in silence,
In his shining cage sat he,
And the day grew dim, but never from him
Came a note of melody.

But late at night in silence
Heart to heart came He and She
To the darkened room; and out of the gloom
Came the linnet's melody.

HEAVE HO!

HEAVE ho! the anchor over the bow,
  And off to sea go I;
The wild wind blows, and nobody knows
  That I have you always nigh.
Right close in my heart I can keep you here
  In memory fond and true,
For there 'll never be one like you, my dear —
  There 'll never be one like you.

Oho! the billows of Biscay Bay,
  And the stars of the southern sea!
But the dark-haired girls may shake their curls,
  With never a look from me;
For the thought of my love shall be ever near,
  Though wide is the ocean blue,
And there 'll never be one like you, my dear —
  There 'll never be one like you.

ROWEN

The end of the world is a weary way,
  And I know not where it lies,
And maidens fair may smile on me there,
  And girls with laughing eyes;
But in all the days of all the year,
  Though I wander the whole world through,
There 'll never be one like you, my dear —
  There 'll never be one like you.

AN OLD-FASHIONED LOVE-SONG

TELL me what within her eyes
   Makes the forgotten Spring arise,
And all the day, if kind she looks,
Flow to a tune like tinkling brooks;
Tell me why, if but her voice
Falls on men's ears, their souls rejoice;
Tell me why, if only she
Doth come into the companie,
All spirits straight enkindled are,
As if a moon lit up a star.

Tell me this that 's writ above,
And I will tell you why I love.

Tell me why the foolish wind
Is to her tresses ever kind,
And only blows them in such wise
As lends her beauty some surprise;

ROWEN

Tell me why no changing year
Can change from Spring, if she appear;
Tell me why to see her face
Begets in all folk else a grace
That makes them fair, as love of her
Did to a gentler nature stir.

Tell me why, if she but go
Alone across the fields of snow,
All fancies of the Springs of old
Within a lover's breast grow bold;
Tell me why, when her he sees,
Within him stirs an April breeze;
And all that in his secret heart
Most sacredly was set apart,
And most was hidden, then awakes,
At the sweet joy her coming makes.

Tell me what is writ above,
And I will tell you why I love.

A LOOK BACK

A CASTLE-YARD—1585

(*Enter* Sir Bevys, *mounted. There comes to meet him, bearing a cup of wine,* Maid Margery)

WHAT, Madge — nay, Madge! why, sweetheart, is it thou?
Faith, but I knew thee not — nor know thee yet!
Madge — Margery — child — coz, thou 'st grown apace.
Why, what a merry coming home is this!
To have my cousin meet me in the court,
My half-grown cousin, grown an angel half,
Lifting a cup to make the wanderer welcome,
With such an arm — why, Margery, 't was a reed,
A meagre, sun-specked reed, when last I saw it,
Three years ago — coz, these were busy years
That dealt so kindly with thee. I set forth
Three years agone last Michaelmas, and thou —

ROWEN

Why, thou and Rupert were an elfish pair
Of freckled striplings — yea, thy elbows, Madge,
My cousin Margery, were as rasping sharp
As old Dame Ursula her tongue — ay, cousin,
I'll drink once more, so thou wilt lift the cup
And show that snowy round again. And Rupert,
My brother Rupert, how fares he? Nay, nay!
First in the tourney? Sturdiest Knight of all?
Gad's grace, the world has wagged while I have wandered.
I'll tell thee this, thou Hebe hazel-eyed,
Had I seen further I had wandered less.
But who'd have thought the slender girl I left,
The straggling weed — thy present grace may pardon
My memory rude — had grown to this fair flower —
To this bright comeliness, this young perfection,
This — this —

   Maid Margery let her lashes down,
And bent her head — perhaps the sunset fell
A trifle 'thwart her face — perhaps she blushed,
As, looking down into the empty cup,
She answered very softly:
    •   · "Rupert did."

PRUDENCE, SPINNING

A STUDIO STUDY

I

PRUDENCE, sitting by the fire,
Lift your head a little higher—
How the firelight ripples in
And out the dimple of your chin—
How your sidewise-tilted head
Snares the flickering gleams of red;
Snares them in a golden net
Than your distaff fleecier yet!
O my Prudence, turn—but no—
Shall a century backward flow?
Prudence—ah, awelladay!
You 're a hundred years away.

ROWEN

II

He who looks upon you hears
Through a hundred bygone years
Whir of wheel and foot's light tap
On the treadle, and the snap
Of the rose-red hickory logs,
Sputtering, sinking on the dogs;
And your breath he almost feels
In a gentle sigh that steals
From your lips, while hand in head
Weave a dream and spin a thread—
Prudence—who'd believe it, pray?
You're a hundred years away.

* * * *

Silent was the studio,
Duller grew the hickory's glow,
And the skylight, cold and faint,
Seemed to frown—"'T is late to paint!"
Prudence drooped a weary head,
Hearing not the painter's tread,
As he crossed the room and bent
Just where blush and firelight blent.
O my Prudence, model fair!
Where's your prim provincial air?
Prudence—ah, awelladay!
How a century slips away!

THE LIGHT

THERE is no shadow where my love is laid;
  For (ever thus I fancy in my dream,
That wakes with me and wakes my sleep) some gleam
Of sunlight, thrusting through the poplar shade,
Falls there; and even when the wind has played
  His requiem for the Day, one stray sunbeam,
  Pale as the palest moonlight glimmers seem,
Keeps sentinel for Her till starlights fade.

And I, remaining here and waiting long,
  And all enfolded in my sorrow's night,
    Who not on earth again her face may see,—
For even memory does her likeness wrong,—
  Am blind and hopeless, only for this light —
    This light, this light, through all the years to be.

WHICH was the harder to lay down,
    Art and ambition, or a crown?
The sceptre or the fiddle-bow?
I know not. All were loath to go.
Yet who would call, did Fate permit,
One of these back to what he quit?

GRANT

SMILE on, thou new-come Spring — if on thy breeze
The breath of a great man go wavering up
And out of this world's knowledge, it is well.

Kindle with thy green flame the stricken trees,
And fire the rose's many-petaled cup,
Let bough and branch with quickening life-blood swell—
But Death shall touch his spirit with a life
That knows not years or seasons. Oh, how small
Thy little hour of bloom! Thy leaves shall fall,
And be the sport of winter winds at strife;
But he has taken on eternity.
Yea, of how much this Death doth set him free! —
Now are we one to love him, once again.
The tie that bound him to our bitterest pain
Draws him more close to Love and Memory.

ROWEN

O Spring, with all thy sweetheart frolics, say,
  Hast thou remembrance of those earlier springs
When we wept answer to the laughing day,
  And turned aside from green and gracious things?
There was a sound of weeping over all—
  Mothers uncomforted, for their sons were not;
  And there was crueler silence: tears grew hot
In the true eyes that would not let them fall.
Up from the South came a great wave of sorrow
  That drowned our hearthstones, splashed with blood our sills;
To-day, that spared, made terrible To-morrow
  With thick presentiment of coming ills.
Only we knew the Right—but oh, how strong,
How pitiless, how insatiable the Wrong!

And then the quivering sword-hilt found a hand
That knew not how to falter or grow weak;
And we looked on, from end to end the land,
And felt the heart spring up, and rise afresh
The blood of courage to the whitened cheek,
And fire of battle thrill the numbing flesh.
Ay, there was death, and pain, and dear ones missed,
And lips forever to grow pale unkissed;
But lo, the man was here, and this was he;
And at his hands Faith gave us victory.

ROWEN

Spring, thy poor life, that mocks his body's death,
Is but a candle's flame, a flower's breath.
He lives in days that suffering made dear
Beyond all garnered beauty of the year.
He lives in all of us that shall outlive
The sensuous things that paltry time can give.
This Spring the spirit of his broken age
   Across the threshold of its anguish stole —
All of him that was noble, fearless, sage,
   Lives in his lovèd nation's strengthened soul.

"LET US HAVE PEACE"

U. S. Grant — July 23, 1885

HIS name was as a sword and shield,
    His words were armèd men,
He mowed his foemen as a field
    Of wheat is mowed — and then
Set his strong hand to make the shorn earth smile again.

Not in the whirlwind of his fight,
    The unbroken line of war,
Did he best battle for the right —
    His victory was more:
Peace was his triumph, greater far than all before.

Who in the spirit and love of peace
    Takes sadly up the blade,
Makes war on war, that wars may cease —
    He striveth undismayed,
And in the eternal strength his mortal strength is stayed.

ROWEN

    Peace, that he conquered for our sake —
        This is his honor, dead.
    We saw the clouds of battle break
        To glory o'er his head —
But brighter shone the light about his dying bed.

    Dead is thy warrior, King of Life,
        Take thou his spirit flown ;
    The prayer of them that knew his strife
        Goes upward to thy throne —
Peace be to him who fought — and fought for Peace alone.

THE BATTLE OF APIA BAY

MARCH 15, 1889

THE portholes black look over the bay
   To the ports on the other side;
And the gun in each grim square porthole dim
   Is guarding a nation's pride.

Two fleets are they in an alien sea,
   And whether as friends or foes,
Till the diplomats' prattle decides their battle,
   Nor sailor nor captain knows.

But strange to each is the sun that starts
   The pitch in the white deck's seams,
While the watch, half dozing with eyes half closing,
   Go home in their waking dreams.

And strange is the land that lies about,
   And the folk with faces brown,
To the Pommerland boy with the yellow beard,
   And the boy from Portland town.

ROWEN

And each looks over the bay to each -
  Is the end of it peace or war?
And the wish that 's best in each brave young breast
  Is the wish for a run ashore.

  *   *   *   *   *

Death came out of the sea last night —
  Death is aboard this morn —
The water is over the war-ship's prow,
  And her snow-white sails are torn.

And the bright blue waves that leap to catch
  The glint of the tropic sun
Roll overhead, and beneath are the dead,
  For the battle is fought and won.

There 's the Pommerland boy with his yellow beard,
  And the Maine boy bearded brown;
And there 's weeping sore on the Pommerland shore;
  There are tears in Portland town.

O ships that guard two nations' pride,
  Death had no need for ye!
They went to their fate through no man's hate —
  Death's servant was the Sea.

WILHELM I., EMPEROR OF GERMANY

MARCH 22, 1797 — JANUARY 2, 1861 — JANUARY 18, 1871 — MARCH 9, 1888

WHEN the gray Emperor at the Gates of Death
    Stood silent, up from Earth there came the sound
Of mourning and dismay; man's futile breath
    Vexed the still air around.

But silent stood the Emperor and alone
Before the ever silent gates of stone
    That open and close at either end of life;
As who, having fought his fight,
Stands, overtaken of night,
    And hears afar the receding sound of strife.

ROWEN

Wide open swing the gates:

Hail, Hohenzollern, hail to thee!
If thou be he
For whom each hero waits,
Hail, hail to thee!

So rings
The chorus of the Kings.
This is the House of Death, the Hall of Fame,
Lit, its vast length, by torches' flickering flame;
And, with their faces by the torch-fires lit,
Around the board the expectant monarchs sit.
Filled are their drink-horns with the immortals' wine —
They wait for him, the latest of their line.

Under the flags they sit, beneath
The which the keen sword spurned its sheath.
Under the flags that first were woven
    To bring the fire to stranger eyes;
That now, at cost of corselets cloven,
    In lines of tattered trophies rise.
To greet the newly come they wait —
The heroes of the German State:

ROWEN

His father, unto whom the west wind blew
The echo of the guns of Waterloo:
That greater FREDERICK, with the lust of power
    Still smoldering in his eyes, his troubled heart
Impatient with the briefness of his hour
    That altered Europe's chart:
And he, the Great Elector, he who first
    Sounded to Poland's King a nation's word:

And he who, earlier, by Rome accursed,
    The trumpet-tone of Martin Luther heard —
      So the long line of faces grim
      Grows faint and dim,
And at the farther end, where lights burn low,
    Where, through a misty glow,
Heroes of German song and story rise
    Gods to our eyes,
Great HERMANN rises, father of a race,
To give the Emperor his place.

  "Come to the table's head,
  Among the ennobled dead!"
He cries: "Nor none shall ask me of thy right."
  Then speaks he to the board:
  "Bow down, in one accord,
To him whose strength is Majesty, not Might.

ROWEN

"Emperor and King he comes; his people's cry
    Pierces our distant sky;
Emperor and King he comes, whose mighty hand
Gathered in one the kingdoms of the land.
    Yet greater far the tale shall be
    That gains him immortality:
To his high task no selfish thought,
No coward hesitance he brought;
All that it was to be a King
    He was, nor counted of the cost.
He rounds our circle — Time may bring
The day when Earth shall need no King —
    All that Kings were, in him Earth lost."

"*Hail, Hohenzollern, hail!*" cried the heroes dead;
And the gray Emperor sat at the table's head.

GENERAL SHERMAN

February 14, 1891

BOWED banners and the drums' thick muffled beat
   For him, and silent crowds along the street;
The stripes of white and crimson on his breast,
And all the trapping of a warrior's rest;
For him the wail of dirges, and the tread
Of the vast army following its dead
Unto the great surrender; half-mast high
For him the flags shall brave the winter sky —
These be his honors: and some old eyes dim
For love's sake, more than fame's — for him, for him!

These things are his; yet not to him alone
Is this proud wealth of ordered honor shown.
Thus to their graves may go all men who stand
Between their country and the foeman's brand:

ROWEN

This is the meed of hardihood in fight,
The formal tribute to a hero's might.
A myriad dead have won the like award—
The unknown, unnumbered servants of the sword.
Hath he no greater honor?

                                                 Yes, although
It win for his dead clay no funeral show,
Nor none shall tell upon the market-place
What gave this hero his most special grace,
That for his memory, in the years to come,
Shall speak more loud than voice of gun or drum.
Great was his soul in fight. But you and I,
Friend, if need be, can set a face to die.
This land of ours has lovers now as then,
Nor shall time coming find her poor in men,
While the strong blood of our old Saxon strain
Fires at the sound of war in pulse and vein.

But this great warrior was in Peace more great,
More noble in his fealty to the state,
More fine in service, in a subtler way
Meeting the vital duty of the day;
Patient and calm, too simply proud to strive
To keep the glory of his past alive.

ROWEN

So burns it still, and shall burn. Every year
Of that high service made him but more dear,
More trusted, more revered. No lust of power
Led him to lengthen out the battle hour;
He sought no office; he would learn no art
To serve him at the polls or in the mart;
And yet he loved the people, nor did pride
Lead him from common joys and cares aside.
His kindly, homely, grizzled face looked down
On all the merrymaking of the town —
A face that we shall miss: we all were proud
When the Old General smiled upon the crowd.
So lived, so died he. Has a great man passed
And left a life more whole unto the last?

Upon the soldier's coffin let this wreath
Tell of his greatest greatness, sword-in-sheath.

LEOPOLD DAMROSCH

FEBRUARY 15, 1885

WAKED at the waving of thy hand, so near
    Came music to the language of the soul —
Not viol alone, or flute: an ordered whole,
That with one voice spoke to us, subtly clear —
So near it came to all that life holds dear,
    So full it was of messages that stole
    Silently to the spirit — of the roll
Of thunders that the heart leaped up to hear —
That we, who look upon the fallen hand
    That shall not rise for music's sake again
        Upon this earth — we, lingering, well may deem
Thee glad with a great joy, to understand,
    At last, the full and all-revealing strain
        That tells what earthly music may but dream.

J. B.

June 7, 1880

THE Actor's dead, and memory alone
　　Recalls the genial magic of his tone;
Marble nor canvas nor the printed page
Shall tell his genius to another age:
A memory, doomed to dwindle less and less,
His world-wide fame shrinks to this littleness.
Yet if, a half a century from to-day,
A tender smile about our old lips play,
And if our grandchild query whence it came,
We 'll say: "A thought of Brougham."—
　　　　　　　　　　　　And that is Fame!

I SERVE *with love a goodly craft,*
And proud thereat am I;
And, if I do but work aright,
Shall never wholly die.

MY SHAKSPERE

WITH beveled binding, with uncut edge,
    With broad white margin and gilded top,
Fit for my library's choicest ledge,
    Fresh from the bindery, smelling of shop,
In tinted cloth, with a strange design —
    Buskin and scroll-work and mask and crown,
    And an arabesque legend tumbling down —
"The Works of Shakspere" were never so fine.
Fresh from the shop! I turn the page —
    Its "ample margin" is wide and fair,
    Its type is chosen with daintiest care;
    There's a "New French Elzevir" strutting there
That would shame its prototypic age.
Fresh from the shop! O Shakspere mine,
I've half a notion you're much too fine!

There's an ancient volume that I recall,
    In foxy leather much chafed and worn;
Its back is broken by many a fall,
    The stitches are loose and the leaves are torn;

ROWEN

And gone is the bastard title, next
    To the title-page scribbled with owners' names,
    That in straggling old-style type proclaims
That the work is from the corrected text
    Left by the late Geo. Steevens, Esquire.

    The broad sky burns like a great blue fire,
And the Lake shines blue as shimmering steel,
    And it cuts the horizon like a blade;
    And behind the poplar's a strip of shade —
    The great tall Lombardy on the lawn.
And, lying there in the grass, I feel
    The wind that blows from the Canada shore,
    And in cool, sweet puffs comes stealing o'er,
    Fresh as any October dawn.

I lie on my breast in the grass, my feet
    Lifted boy-fashion, and swinging free,
    The old brown Shakspere in front of me.
And big are my eyes, and my heart's a-beat;
And my whole soul's lost — in what? — who knows?
Perdita's charms or Perdita's woes —
Perdita fairy-like, fair and sweet.
    Is any one jealous, I wonder, now,
    Of my love for Perdita? For I vow
    I loved her well. And who can say
    That life would be quite the same life to-day —

ROWEN

That Love would mean so much, if she
Had not taught me its A B C?

The Grandmother, thin and bent and old,
    But her hair still dark and her eyes still bright,
        Totters around among the flowers —
Old-fashioned flowers of pink and white;
And turns with a trowel the dark rich mold
    That feeds the blooms of her heart's delight.
        Ah me! for her and for me the hours
Go by, and for her the smell of earth —
And for me the breeze and a far love's birth,
    And the sun and the sky and all the things
    That a boy's heart hopes and a poet sings.

Fresh from the shop! O Shakspere mine,
It was n't the binding made you divine!
I knew you first in a foxy brown,
In the old, old home, where I laid me down,
    In the idle summer afternoons,
With you alone in the odorous grass,
    And set your thoughts to the wind's low tunes,
And saw your children rise up and pass —
And dreamed and dreamed of the things to be,
Known only, I think, to you and me.

I 've hardly a heart for you dressed so fine —
Fresh from the shop, O Shakspere mine!

ON SEEING MAURICE LELOIR'S ILLUSTRATIONS TO STERNE'S "SENTIMENTAL JOURNEY"

LELOIR, what kinship lies between you two —
This century-vanished Englishman and you? —
You who can lead us, grateful in surprise,
All that he saw to see with trusting eyes —
Nay, at your beck his head peeps, gaunt and hoar,
Out of the window in the po'chaise door.

Is it not this: birth made him of your race
(Though Clonmel and not Calais were the place,)
If heart and fancy be the best of birth?

Some day, Leloir, your spirit, freed from earth,
Walking that special heaven set apart
For those who made religion of their art,
Will meet this elder friend, and he will turn
And speak to you in French — this Laurence Sterne.

TO A READER OF THE XXIst CENTURY

YOU, when you read this book, shall find
How You or We have fallen behind.
Where'er you be, I know you not;
But, if my memory be forgot,
Remember, proud of life and thought
Though *You* may strut, *I* hold you naught.
You *are* not yet — you *may be* — still,
How do I know you ever *will?*

But yet I hope, in future days,
You may exist, to cast your gaze
Round some old bibliomaniac's room,
Shrouded in sober russet gloom,
And let it fall upon this book;
Then turn this page — I 'll catch your look.

Aye! though the while this line you read
A coverlet of daisy brede
Shall lie my old-time bed above
And all that was my life and love;

ROWEN

I speak to you from out a day
When *I*, not *You*, can see the Play,
And find the stage's mimicry
More real than are *You* to *Me*.
When blood went slipping through this heart,
I saw it all — I was a part.

This is our day — you turn the page,
And see the pictures of our age.
"A treasure!" cries your bibliopole,
With fervor in his musty soul:
"A Daly private print — a chaste
Example of our fathers' taste.
They made books *then* — who can, in our
Degenerate days of — magnet — power?
See — Ada Rehan, Fisher, Drew,
Dame Gilbert, Lewis — through and through
The sharp-cut plates are clear as new!"
Then comes the old, the tardy praise —
"Those were the drama's palmy days."

But We? You'll see the shadow — now
To us these living creatures bow,
For us they smile — for us they feign
Or love or hatred, joy or pain;
For us this white breast heaves — this voice
Makes hearts too young too much rejoice;

ROWEN

For us those splendid eyes are lit;
For us awakes embodied wit;
For us the music and the light —
The listening faces, flushed and bright;
The glow, the passion, and the dream —
To you — how far it all must seem!

You know the names — but we behold,
In sweet old age that is not old,
Though Time play tricks with face and hair,
Our Gentlewoman past compare.
We see her deftly thread the set
Old figures of the minuet;
We see her Partner's snow-crowned face
Bent o'er her hand in antique grace.

You know the names — before our eyes
Proud Katherine's anger flames and dies;
For us Petruchio pays his court;
For us the high tempestuous port,
Lowered at last in humble, sweet
Submission at a husband's feet.
You know the names — but ah! who hears
The laughter when one face appears?

You know the names — but what are they?
We know the folk that make the Play!

ROWEN

Love's merry Up, Love's doleful Down,
The fickle fashion of the town
Take form and shape for us, and show
To heart and eye the world we know.

You have the pictures, and the names
That are but Yours as they are Fame's;
See them, O dim Potential Shade,
Even as we see them now arrayed:
Try to put nature's vital hue
Into the faces that you view;
And think, while Fancy labors thus,
This all is breathing Life to Us.

FOR AN OLD POET

WHEN he is old and past all singing,
    Grant, kindly Time, that he may hear
The rhythm through joyous Nature ringing,
    Uncaught by any duller ear.

Grant that, in memory's deeps still cherished,
    Once more may murmur low to him
The winds that sung in years long perished,
    Lit by the suns of days grown dim.

Grant that the hours when first he listened
    To bird-songs manhood may not know,
In fields whose dew for lovers glistened,
    May come back to him ere he go.

Grant only this, O Time most kindly,
    That he may hear the song you sung
When love was new—and, harkening blindly,
    Feign his o'er-wearied spirit young.

With sound of rivers singing round him,
    On waves that long since flowed away,
Oh, leave him, Time, where first Love found him,
    Dreaming To-morrow in To-day!

WILKIE COLLINS

September 23, 1889

WHEN Arabs sat around
    And heard the Thousand Nights —
Beyond the tent's close bound,
    Beyond the watch-fire lights —
Their believing spirits flew
    To a land where strange things seem
As simple things and true,
    And the best truth is a dream.

And when the tale was told —
    Genie and Princess fair
Brought to an end — their gold
    They sought, with an absent air;
And dropped it at His feet
    Who had led to the land of Delight;
And, dreaming of Princesses sweet,
    They passed out into the night.

ROWEN

So, still under your spell,
   Teller of magic tales,
These lines I would fain let tell
   The debt whose payment fails.
Take them: if they were gold
   'T would but discharge a due —
And, for the tales you told,
   I shall remember you.

FOR C. J. T., CONCERNING A. D.

HERE shall you see the sweetest mind
That loves our simpler humankind:
The things that touch your heart and mine
He knows by sympathy so fine
That he, an alien, over sea,
Partner in our best thought can be.
Not the ATLANTIC'S swell and moan
Can part his fancy from our own.

* * * *

See but a child with wistful eyes
THE DOCTOR'S gloomy windows rise,
And that sad comedy is played
That makes us love one little maid:
See the kind face we children knew,
And PRUDENCE is our "Aunty," too;
Think of the madcap loves of youth,
And think of BELL, LOUISE, and RUTH:
Think of the loves not Love, alas!
And of ROSINE in Mont Parnasse:
Dream of the things most sweet and true
That your best moments bring to you,
And find this gentle Poet's art
Voices the thought that stirred your heart.

EDMUND CLARENCE STEDMAN

THOUGH to his song the reeds respondent rustle
    That cradled Pan what time all song was young,
Though in a new world city's restless bustle
    He sounds a lyre in fields Sicilian strung;
Though his the power the days of old to waken,
    Though Nature's melody 's as clear to him
As ere of dryads were the woods forsaken,
    And the fresh world of myth grew faint and dim —
A dearer grace is his when men's eyes glisten
    With closer sympathies his page above,
And near his spirit draws to hearts that listen
    The song that sweetly rounds with Home and Love.

NEW YORK, December 10, 1884.

AN EPISTLE

To Master Brander Matthews, Writer, on the Occasion of his Putting Forth a Book entitled "Pen and Ink"

   New London, Conn., Sept. 10, 1888.
Dear Brander:
    I have known thee long, and found
Thee wise in council, and of judgment sound;
Steadfast in friendship, sound and clear in wit,
And more in virtues than may here be writ.
But most I joy, in these machine-made days,
To see thee constant in a craftsman's ways;
That the plain tool that knew thy 'prentice hand
Gathers no rust upon thy writing-stand;
That no Invention saves the labor due
To any Task that's worth the going through;
That now when butter snubs the stranger churn,
Plain pen and ink still serve a writer's turn.
Though I, more firmly orthodox, still hold,
In dire default of quills, to steel or gold,
And though thy pen be rubber — let it pass —
A breath of blemish on thy soul's clear glass.

ROWEN

There is no "writing fluid" in thy pot,
But honest ink of nutgall brew, God wot!
Thou dost not an electric needle ply,
And, like a housewife with an apple-pie,
Prick thy fair page into a stencil-plate—
Then daub with lampblack for a duplicate.
Nor thine the sloven page whereon the shirk
With the rough tool attempts the finished work,
And introduces to the sight of men
The Valet Pencil for the Master Pen.

Not all like thee, in this uneasy age,
When more by trick than toil we earn our wage!
Here by the sea a gentle poet dwells,
And in fair leisure weaves his magic spells;
And yet doth dare with countenance serene
To weave them on a tinkling steel machine,
Where an impertinent and soulless bell
Rings, at each finished line, a jangling knell.
The muse and I, we love him, and I think
She may forgive his slight to pen and ink,
And let no dull mechanic cam or cog
The lightsome movement of his metres clog;
But oh! I grieve to see his fingers toy
With this base slave in dalliance close and coy,

ROWEN

*While in his standish dries the atrid spring
Where hides the shyer muse that loves to sing.
Give me the old-time ink, black, flowing, free,
And give, oh, give! the old goose-quill to me —
The goose-quill, whispering of humility.
It whispers to the bard: "Fly not too high!
You flap your wings — remember, so could I.
I cackled in my life-time, it is true;
But yet again remember, so do You.
And there were some things possible to me
That possible to you will never be.
I stood for hours on one columnar leg,
And, if my sex were such, could lay an egg.
Oh, well for you, if you could thus beget
Material for your morning omelette;
Or, if things came to such a desperate pass,
You could in calm contentment nibble grass!
Conceited bard! and can you sink to rest
Upon the feather-pillow of your breast?"*

*Hold, my dear Brander, to your pot of ink:
The muse sits poised upon that fountain's brink.
And that you long may live to hold a pen
I'll breathe a prayer;*
    The world will say "Amen!"

ON READING CERTAIN PUBLISHED
LETTERS OF W. M. T.

IT is as though the gates of heaven swung,
    Once only, backward, and a spirit shone
Upon us, with a face to which there clung
    Naught of that mortal veil which sore belies,
    But looked such love from such high-changèd eyes,
That, even from earth, we knew them for his own.

Knew them for his, and marveled; for he came
    Among us, and went from us, and we knew
Only the smoke and ash that hid the flame,
    Only the cloak and vestment of his soul;
    And knew his priesthood only by his stole —
And, thus unknown, he went his journey through.

Yet there were some who knew him, though his face
    Was never seen by them; although his hand
Lay never warm in theirs, they yet had grace
    To see, past all misjudgment; his true heart
    Throbbed for them in the creatures of his art,
And they could read his words, and understand.

ROWEN

All men may know him now, and know how kind
    The hand in chastisement so sure and strong —
All men may know him now, and dullards blind
    Into the secrets of his soul may see;
    And all shall love — but, Steadfast Greatheart, we,
We knew thee when the wide world did thee wrong.

SAYS the Man in the Moon, "It's a fine world there";
　But he wonders how it can please us
To walk with our heads hanging down in the air —
　For that is the way he sees us.

CHAKEY EINSTEIN

PHARAOH, King of Egypt's land,
 Held you in his cruel hand,
Till the Appointed of the Lord
Led you forth and drowned his horde.
Cushan, Eglon's Moabites,
Jabin, then the Midianites,
Ammonite and Philistine
Held you, by decree divine.
Shishak spoiled you — but the list
Fades in dim tradition's mist —
And on history's page we see
One long tale of misery,
Century after century through —
Chains and lashes for the Jew.
Haman and Antiochus,
Herod, Roman Socius,
Spoiled you, crushed you, various ways,
Till the dawn of Christian days;

ROWEN

Since which time your wrongs and shame
Have remained about the same.
Whipped and chained, your teeth pulled out;
English cat and Russian knout
Made familiar with your back —
When you were n't upon the rack —
Marked for scorn of Christian men;
Pilfered, taxed, and taxed again;
Pilloried, prisoned, burnt and stoned,
Stripped of even the clothes you owned;
Child of Torture, Son of Shame,
Robbed of even a father's name —
In this year of Christian grace,
What 's your state and what 's your place?
Why you 're rich and strong and gay —
Chakey Einstein, owff Browdway!

Myriad signs along the street
Israelitish names repeat.
Lichtenstein and Morgenroth
Sell the pants and sell the coat;
Minzesheimer, Isaacs, Meyer,
Levy, Lehman, Simon, Speyer —
These may just suggest a few
Specimens of Broadway Jew —

ROWEN

And these gentlemen have made
Quite their own the Dry-gootz Trade.
Surely you 're on top to-day,
Chakey Einstein, owff Browdway.

Fat and rich you are, and loud;
Fond of being in a crowd;
Fond of diamonds and rings;
Fond of haberdashers' things;
Fond of color, fond of noise;
Fond of treating "owl der boys"
(Yet, it 's only fair to state,
For yourself, most temperate);
Fond of women, fond of song;
Fond of bad cigars, and strong;
Fond, too much, of Brighton's Race
(Where you 're wholly out of place,
For no Jew in Time's long course
Knew one thing about a horse);
Fond of life, and fond of fun
(Once your "beezness" wholly done);
Open-handed, generous, free,
Full of Christian charity
(Far more full than he who pokes
At your avarice his jokes);

ROWEN

Fond of friends, and ever kind
To the sick and lame and blind
(And, though loud you else may be,
Silent in your charity);
Fond of Mrs. Einstein and
Her too-numerous infant band,
Ever willing they should share
Your enjoyment everywhere —
What of you is left to say,
Chakey Einstein, owff Browdway?

Though you 're spurned in some hotels,
You have kin among the swells —
Great musicians, poets true,
Painters, singers not a few,
Own their cousinship to you:
And all England, so they say,
Yearly blooms on Primrose Day
All in memory of a Jew
Of the self-same race as you;
Greatest leader ever known
Since the Queen came to her throne;
Bismarck's only equal foe,
With a thrust for every blow,
One who rose from place to place
To lead the Anglo-Saxon race,

ROWEN

One whose statecraft wise and keen
Made an Empress of a Queen —
You 've your share in Primrose Day,
Chakey Einstein, owff Browdway!

Well, good friend, we look at you
And behold the Conquering Jew:
In despite of all the years
Filled with agonies and fears;
In despite of stake and chain;
In despite of Rome and Spain;
'Spite of prison, rack, and lash,
You are here, and you 've the cash:
You are Trade's uncrownèd king —
You are mostly everything —
Only one small joke, O Jew!
Has the Christian world on you —
When your son, your first-born boy,
Solomon, your fond heart's joy,
Grows to manhood's years, he 'll wed
One a Christian born and bred;
Blue of blood, of lineage old,
Who will take him for his gold —
That 's not all — so far the joke
Is upon the Christian folk.

ROWEN

But, dear Chakey, when he goes
In his proper Sabbath clo'es,
To the House of Worship, he
And his little family,
He will pass the synagogue,
And upon his way will jog
To a Church, wherein his pew
Will bear a name unknown to you —
One quite unknown in old B'nai B'rith —
Eynston maybe — maybe Smith.
That's just as sure as day is day —
Chakey Einstein, owff Browdway!

A FABLE FOR RULERS

(FROM THE FRENCH)

A KING of Persia, once upon a day,
Rode with his courtiers to the chase away.
Thirst o'ertook him in a desert plain,
Where he sought a cooling fount in vain.
Last he chanced upon a garden fine,
Rich in luscious orange, grape, and pine:
"God forbid my thirst I slake!"
Quoth he, "for the owner's sake.
For if to pluck one single fruit I dare,
These my viziers will lay the garden bare."

BISMARCK SOLILOQUIZES

THE German Emperor—that 's his title—not
The one that (thanks to me) his Grandsire got.—
Emperor of Germany served his father's turn;
'T will not serve his. Well, well, we live and learn.
I, in my age, have learned one certain thing:
Who makes a king shall perish by a king.

What else should come of making kings? The best
Is but a Policy in purple drest.
I hatched this Policy within my brain:
But shall it hatch a Policy again?
I made an Emperor; made his heir, and he
Has made an Emperor to make mock of me.

Is this the way God laughs at men? to spoil
Their work, and bring to nothingness their toil?
To give the seed, the wit to make it grow,
Patience to nurse this tree till blossoms blow,

ROWEN

To lend the fatness of the labored land,
And turn the fruit to dust within the hand?
If so — His ways shall not be understood —
Let me laugh, too. Surely the jest is good
I have time for laughing now. In days gone by
We had no laughing-times, my kings and I:
Nor did I dream such gratitude was theirs
To save my latter years from statecraft's cares,
And let me sit in calm retirement down
To watch a youthful Emperor play the clown!

Right well you play it, William mine — how well,
It takes a critic old as I to tell.
No madder jest a merry mind could plan
Than Kings coquetting with the Laboring Man.
A gay conceit, indeed, it seems to me —
That Congress, summoned by your high decree
To view the woes of man, and find a cure
For you to guarantee as swift and sure.
Nor did your humor miss a happy chance
When you dispatched your Mother into France.
Of course, to give the joke its subtle sting,
A Grandmother would be the proper thing.
Still, 't was amusing — and instructive, since
It shows just what can make a Frenchman wince,

ROWEN

Make his lip quiver and his thin cheek blanch —
A conqueror's widow with an olive branch.
Oh, had she gone — the jest to carry through —
To see if sparks still lingered at St. Cloud!
Play your game out, boy: I will look and laugh.
Thresh over the poor wheat I threshed to chaff.
Learn the hard lesson I so long have known,
That steel's the only metal for a throne.
You are — your guns, and nothing else on earth,
Except the brutal accident of birth.
Think you the golden years will come again
When the poor peasants, fleeing from the plain,
Huddled beneath the castle walls, stretched hands
To pray the War Lord to protect their lands
Against the alien plunderer, kissed the sod,
And thought him regent of Almighty God?
Why, child, that dogma of your heaven-sent right
Is, in this day, a mere excuse polite
For owning cannon; and the more you own
The more divine your right is to the throne.
Think you these people whose intelligence
Fills you with proud paternal confidence
Have learned — you let them learn — to write and read,
To find out ways of bettering their breed —
Yet hold themselves still made for you to bleed?

ROWEN

And does the spider educate the fly,
Teaching him: "By this belly know that I
Can chain you; this my glittering web is set
To hold your feet fast in a sticky net.
So, now, walk in, I pray. Divinest Right
Has given me a pretty appetite!"
Madman and babe — you send your fly to school;
And then expect your fly to be your fool!

Play on, play on! *I* kept your "right" alive;
I made a medieval dogma thrive
On barren modern soil; but *my* War Lord
In one hand bore a whip; in one a sword.
His Right men held Divine; his title clear —
Through gratitude? through love? — hope? —
      Fool! through Fear!

IMITATION

MY love she leans from the window
    Afar in a rosy land;
And red as a rose are her blushes,
    And white as a rose her hand.

And the roses cluster around her,
    And mimic her tender grace;
And nothing but roses can blossom
    Wherever she shows her face.

I dwell in a land of winter,
    From my love a world apart —
But the snow blooms over with roses
    At the thought of her in my heart.

* * * * *

This German style of poem
    Is uncommonly popular now;
For the worst of us poets can do it —
    Since Heine showed us how.

"MAGDALENA"

SAT we 'neath the dark verandah,
   Years and years ago;
And I softly pressed a hand a
   Deal more white than snow.
And I cast aside my *reina*,
   As I gazed upon her face,
And I read her "Magdalena,"
   While she smoothed her Spanish lace —
Read her Waller's "Magdalena"—
   She had Magdalena's grace.
Read her of the Spanish duel,
Of the brother, courtly, cruel,
Who between the British wooer
   And the Seville lady came;
How her lover promptly slew her
   Brother, and then fled in shame —
How he dreamed, in long years after,
Of the river's rippling laughter —

ROWEN

    Of the love he used to know
In the myrtle-curtained villa
Near the city of Sevilla
    Years and years ago.

Ah, how warmly was I reading,
    As I gazed upon her face!
And my voice took tones of pleading,
    For I sought to win her grace.
Surely, thought I, in her veins
Runs some drop of foreign strains —
There is something half Castilian
In that lip that shames vermilion;
In that mass of raven tresses,
Tossing like a falcon's jesses;
In that eye with trailing lashes,
And its witching upward flashes —
    Such, indeed, I know,
Shone where Guadalquivir plashes
    Years and years ago.

Looking in her face I read it —
    How the metre trips! —
And the god of lovers sped it
    On my happy lips —

ROWEN

All those words of mystic sweetness
Spoke I with an airy neatness,
As I never had before —
As I cannot speak them more —
Reja, plaza, and mantilla,
"No palabras" and Sevilla,
Caballero and sombrero,
And duenna and Duero,
Spada, señor, sabe Dios —
Smooth as pipe of Melibœus —
Ah, how very well I read it,
    Looking in her lovely eyes!
When 't was o'er, I looked for credit,
    As she softly moved to rise.

*   *   *   *   *

Doting dream, ah, dream fallacious —
    Years and years ago! —
For she only said: "My gracious —
    What a lot of French you know!"

MAY the light of some morning skies
In days when the sun knew how to rise,
Stay with my spirit until I go
To be the boy that I used to know.

"ONE, TWO, THREE!"

IT was an old, old, old, old lady,
    And a boy that was half-past three;
And the way that they played together
    Was beautiful to see.

She could n't go running and jumping,
    And the boy, no more could he;
For he was a thin little fellow,
    With a thin little twisted knee.

They sat in the yellow sunlight,
    Out under the maple-tree;
And the game that they played I 'll tell you,
    Just as it was told to me.

It was Hide-and-Go-Seek they were playing,
    Though you 'd never have known it to be—
With an old, old, old, old lady,
    And a boy with a twisted knee.

ROWEN

The boy would bend his face down
    On his one little sound right knee,
And he'd guess where she was hiding,
    In guesses One, Two, Three!

"You are in the china-closet!"
    He would cry, and laugh with glee —
It was n't the china-closet;
    But he still had Two and Three.

"You are up in Papa's big bedroom,
    In the chest with the queer old key!"
And she said: "You are *warm* and *warmer;*
    But you 're not quite right," said she.

"It can't be the little cupboard
    Where Mama's things used to be —
So it must be the clothes-press, Gran'ma!".
    And he found her with his Three.

Then she covered her face with her fingers,
    That were wrinkled and white and wee,
And she guessed where the boy was hiding,
    With a One and a Two and a Three.

ROWEN

And they never had stirred from their places,
    Right under the maple-tree—
This old, old, old, old lady,
    And the boy with the lame little knee—
This dear, dear, dear old lady,
    And the boy who was half-past three.

THE LITTLE SHOP

Air: The Bailiff's Daughter of Islington

I KNOW a shop, and a funny little shop,
    In a street that lies anigh;
And I saw the sign set on the door,
    One day as I went by.
And oh! it was so poor and small
    I could not help but stop,
As you would stop, if you should come
    On such a little shop.

I went inside, and found a little boy,
    Far older, I am sure, than I;
He said to me: "Kind sir, what toy
    Will you kindly be pleased to buy?"
And I bought a horse that was painted so red
    As never was charger yet;
One penny, one penny was all I paid
    That splendid horse to get.

ROWEN

For pity of them that were so poor
    I bought me a host of things:
A Noah's Ark without a roof;
    A dove without its wings;
A little trumpet made of tin,
    That cost a single cent —
And all the time that little boy
    Knew just how my money went.

He was, oh! so old, this funny little boy,
    And so sober and so kind:
He sold a five-cent doll for three,
    Because one eye was blind.
And, oh! how proud he was to sell
    Each poor and petty toy,
For he was left to keep the shop,
    This poor little old-time boy.

There is a babe, and a well-beloved babe,
    A babe that belongs to me;
I brought her home these penny toys
    To deck her Christmas tree.
And on that Christmas tree there hung
    A world of trifles fair,
For all the folk that love her well
    Had set their kindness there.

ROWEN

But of all the toys, of all the many toys,
    Was naught that pleased her mind
Except the trumpet made of tin,
    And the doll with one eye blind.
And best of all that Christmas brought,
    She held one little toy
That I bought for a cent in the little shop,
    To please that aged boy.

GRANDFATHER WATTS'S PRIVATE FOURTH

GRANDFATHER WATTS used to tell us boys
That a Fourth wa'n't a Fourth without any noise.
He would say, with a thump of his hickory stick,
That it made an American right down *sick*
To see his sons on the Nation's Day
Sit round, in a sort of a listless way,
With no oration and no train-band,
No fire-work show and no root-beer stand;
While his grandsons, before they were out of bibs,
Were ashamed — Great Scott! — to fire off squibs.

And so, each Independence morn,
Grandfather Watts took his powder-horn,
And the flint-lock shot-gun *his* father had
When he fought under Schuyler, a country lad;

ROWEN

And Grandfather Watts would start and tramp
Ten miles to the woods at Beaver Camp;
For Grandfather Watts used to say — and scowl —
That a decent chipmunk, or woodchuck, or owl
Was better company, friendly or shy,
Than folks who did n't keep Fourth of July.
And so he would pull his hat down on his brow,
And march for the woods, sou'-east by sou'.

But once — ah, long, long years ago, —
For Grandfather 's gone where good men go, —
One hot, hot Fourth, by ways of our own
(Such short-cuts as boys have always known),
We hurried, and followed the dear old man
Beyond where the wilderness began —
To the deep black woods at the foot of the Hump;
And there was a clearing — and a stump.

A stump in the heart of a great wide wood,
And there on that stump our Grandfather stood,
Talking and shouting out there in the sun,
And firing that funny old flint-lock gun
Once in a minute — his head all bare —
Having his Fourth of July out there:
The Fourth of July that he used to know,
Back in eighteen-and-twenty or so!

ROWEN

First, with his face to the heavens blue,
He read the "Declaration" through;
And then, with gestures to left and right,
He made an oration erudite,
Full of words six syllables long —
And then our Grandfather burst into song!
And, scaring the squirrels in the trees,
Gave "Hail, Columbia!" to the breeze.

*And I tell you the old man never heard
When we joined in the chorus, word for word!
But he sang out strong to the bright blue sky;
And if voices joined in his Fourth of July,
He heard them as echoes from days gone by.*

And when he had done, we all slipped back,
As still as we came, on our twisting track,
While words more clear than the flint-lock shots
Rang in our ears.   And Grandfather Watts?

He shouldered the gun his father bore,
And marched off home, nor'-west by nor'.

TO MY DAUGHTER

CONCERNING A BUNCH OF BLOSSOMS

THE blossoms she gave him — indeed, they were fair;
And grateful the odor they cast on the air;
And he put them in water, and set them anigh
His little round window that looked on the sky.
And the blush of those blossoms, their pleasant perfume,
Made a sweet little spot in that dull little room —
Made a sweet little spot for a day and an hour;
Then —
      Well, little Lil, what 's the fate of a flower?

The blossoms she gave him — indeed, they were fair;
But I think that the least of the giving was there,
In that vase by the window — the look in her face —
Her tender and youthful and delicate grace —

ROWEN

The voice that just trembled in gentle replies,
The look and the light in her uplifted eyes —
Ah! these to my thinking were dearer by far
Than ever the fairest of May-blossoms are.

The blossoms she gave him — you ask, little Lil,
With a lip that is quivering and blue eyes that fill —
If they faded?
               They did — but there's no need to cry!
For they blossomed again where I can't have them die —
These roseate tints on your soft little cheek,
In a manner mysterious certainly speak
Of a bunch of pink blossoms, fresh torn from the tree,
That in eighteen-and-eighty your mother gave me.

SCHUBERT'S KINDER-SCENEN

THE spirit of the Ingle Nook
    Has come to lead me forth,
To wonder at the leaping brook —
    The wind from out the north.

To wander with Haroun the Great
    Through groves of Eastern scent;
To watch beyond the garden gate
    The birds fly, heavenward bent;

To lie amid the grass, and dream
    Each slim and spreading spire
A tufted palm, lit by the gleam
    Of distant heavens' fire.

To dream and dream of things beyond
    The gate — beyond to-day —
Until upon the miller's pond
    The low red light shall play.

ROWEN

And then, when all my dreams shall swim
    To murmuring of the brook,
I shall be led from twilight dim
    Back to the Ingle Nook.

BALLADS OF THE TOWN

AND LATER LYRICS

[1896]

BALLADS OF THE TOWN

I. THE MAID OF MURRAY HILL

SAINT VALENTINE, Saint Valentine!
    I love a maid of New York town,
And every day, on my homeward way,
    She walks the Avenue down.
At five o'clock, dear Saint, she goes
    Tripping down Murray Hill,
And the hands of the clock in the old brick spire
    Stand still, stand still, stand still!

Saint Valentine, Saint Valentine!
    Oh, could you know how fair a maid —
So trim of dress, and so gold of tress,
    You'd know why I'm afraid.
I see her pass, I smile and bow,
    As I go up Murray Hill,
And I say to a foolish hope of mine:
    Be still, be still, be still!

Saint Valentine, Saint Valentine,
    Oh, could you see how close her gown
Binds tight and warm about her form,
    This maid of New York town,
You 'd know a mountain would to me
    Be less than Murray Hill,
If only around her my arm could slip,
    And she 'd stand still, stand still.

Saint Valentine, Saint Valentine!
    She is so fair, so rich, so great,
I have no right to think what might
    Be this poor clerk's estate.
And yet the bells in yon brick spire,
    As we pass on Murray Hill,
They ring, they ring — she 's not for me —
    And still — and still — and still —

II. THE FRIVOLOUS GIRL

HER silken gown it rustles
    As she goes down the stair;
And in all the place there 's ne'er a face
    One half, one half so fair.
But, oh! I saw her yesterday —
    And no one knew 't was she —
When a little sick child looked up and smiled
    As she sat on my lady's knee.

Her fan it flirts and flutters,
    Her eyes grow bright — grow dim —
And all around no man is found
    But thinks she thinks of him.
But, oh! to her the best of all,
    Though they be great and grand,
Are less than the sick whose smiles come quick
    At the touch of my lady's hand.

Her little shoe of satin
  Peeps underneath her skirt —
And a foot so small ought never at all
  To move in mire and dirt.
But, oh! she goes among the poor,
  And heavy hearts rejoice —
As they can tell who know her well —
  To hear my lady's voice.

Her glove is soft as feathers
  Upon the nestling dove;
Its touch so light I have no right
  To think, to dream of love —
But, oh! when, clad in simplest garb,
  She goes where none may see,
I watch, and pray that some happy day
  My lady may pity ME.

III. KITTY'S SUMMERING

HAVE you seen e'er a sign of my Kitty?
 Have you seen a fair maiden go by
Who was wed in this summer-struck city
 About the first week in July?
  How fair was her face there 's no telling;
   She was well-nigh as wealthy as fair,
  And of marble and brick was her dwelling
   On the North side of Washington Square.

Have you seen her at *Newport* a-driving?
 Have you seen her a-flirt at the *Pier?*
Is she written among the arriving
 At the *Shoals* or the *Hamptons* this year?
  Or out where the ocean bird flutters
   Are the sea-breezes tossing her hair?
  For closed are the ancient green shutters
   In the house on North Washington Square.

BALLADS OF THE TOWN

So you, too, are trying to find her?
  Then climb up these stairways with me,
That twist and grow blinder and blinder,
  Till the skylight near heaven you see.
    Is the sun my dull studio gilding?
      Ah, no, it is Kitty sits there —
She has moved to the Studio Building
  On the SOUTH side of Washington Square.

IV. AT DANCING SCHOOL

THE master 's old and lean and grim,
    And the gout is in his knees;
And though he says his eyes are dim,
    My smallest fault he sees.
        Chassez and bow, and turn and bow —
            I try my best to please —
        No matter how, there's a frown on his brow —
            And the gout is in his knees.

He taught my father long ago;
    He teaches me to-day:
A thousand small tired feet, I know,
    Have stirred at his "chassez!"
        Chassez and bow, and turn and bow —
            To the girl in pink and gray —
        No matter how, there 's a frown on his brow,
            As he teaches me to-day.

But what care I how stern he be,
  If Pink-and-Gray be kind?
Oh, let him frown his best on me
  If so he have a mind.
    Chassez and bow, and turn and bow —
      My happy eyes are blind
    To the frown on his brow — no matter how —
      If Pink-and-Gray be kind.

Oh, let him frown, and frown his fill,
  Howe'er he make me stir;
The CALEDONIAN QUADRILLE
  To-day I dance with her.
    Chassez and bow, and turn and bow —
      The fiddles whizz and whirr.
    No matter how be the frown on his brow,
      To-day I dance with her.

* * * * * * * * *

Ah, me! What years have slid away,
  Sweet Pink-and-Gray, and *how!*
Since that old "CALEDONIAN'S" day —
  They do not dance it now.
    Chassez and bow, and turn and bow;
      And the master, grim and gray,
    Has a frown on his brow, and yet, somehow,
      The scholars slip away.

I sit here in the evening's cool,
  And see you, Pink-and-Gray,
Lead children to the dancing-school —
  To the master grim and gray.
    Chassez and bow, and turn and bow —
    I might have walked to-day —
    No matter how — 't will never be now —
    With you, sweet Pink-and-Gray!

V. THEIR WEDDING JOURNEY — 1834

DEAR MOTHER,
    When the Coach rolled off
 From dear old Battery Place
I hid my face within my hands —
 That is, I hid my face.
Tom says *(he 's leaning over me!)*
 'T was on his Shoulder, too;
But, oh, I pray you will believe
 I wept to part from You.

And when we rattled up Broadway
 I wept to leave the Scene
Familiar to my happy Youth
 (I did love Bowling Green).
I wept at Slidell's Chandlery
 To see the smoak arise —
'T was only at the City Hall
 Tom bade me wipe my Eyes.

BALLADS OF THE TOWN

By Mr. Niblo's Garden, where
    You would not let me go,
We went, and travell'd up the Hill —
    So fast, and yet so slow!
And so we left behind the Town
    And ere the Sun had set
We reach'd the Inn at Tubby Hook — 5
We have not left it yet!

I know that we are very Wrong —
    Dear Mother, pray forgive!
From Sun to Sun 't is all so sweet —
    It seems so sweet to Live!
I know the things we meant to do,
    The road we vow'd to go,
But Tom and I are here, and — oh,
    Dear Mother, *do* you know?

We have not gone to Uncle John's,
    Though Yonkers is so near —
We never shall see Cousin Van
    At Tarrytown, I fear.
Our Peekskill friends, the Fishkill folk,
    And all the waiting rest —
Tom bids me tell you they may wait —
    (He says they may be Blest).

I know 't is ill to linger here
  Hid in this woodland Inn,
When all along Queen Anne's broad road
  Await our Friends and Kin;
But, Dear Mama (when I was small
  You let me call you so),
'T is such Felicity and Joy
  With Him, Here! Do you know?
                    YOUR ISABEL.
P. S.— Tom sends
  His love. Please write, "*I know.*"

VI. TO A JUNE BREEZE

BEING A LOVER'S MESSAGE TO HIS MISTRESS
A-SUMMERING

WIND of the City Streets,
    Impatient to be free,
In this dull time of heats
    My love takes wings to flee —
Leave thou this idle Town
And hunt Her down.

    Wherever She may stay,
        By Sea or Mountain-side,
    Make thou thy airy Way,
        If there She bide;
    If sea-spray kiss Her face;
    Or hills find grace.

And, having found Her out,
    On Sands or under Trees,
Say that I wait in doubt,
    To melt with love or freeze:
Nor yet hath Summer stirred;
But waits Her word.

    Say that, if She so please,
        These ways so dusty-dry,
    With their poor song-shunn'd Trees,
        Shall ring with Melody;
    And turn Love's Wilderness,
    If She say Yes.

But if my Fate fall so
    That She will naught of me,
Tell Her the Winter's snow
    Shall strip the greenest tree:
One only Frost I fear —
She makes my Year.

    Go, then, sweet Wind, and pray
        That She remember
    She makes my March or May,
        June or December —

BALLADS OF THE TOWN

If Town grow green with trees:·
If the new Blossoms freeze:
    Hers it is but to say —
Pray Her that so She please —
    Pray Her remember!

VII. THE CHAPERON

I TAKE my chaperon to the play —
    She thinks she 's taking me.
And the gilded youth who owns the box,
    A proud young man is he —
But how would his young heart be hurt
    If he could only know
    That not for his sweet sake I go
    Nor yet to see the trifling show;
But to see my chaperon flirt.

Her eyes beneath her snowy hair
    They sparkle young as mine;
There 's scarce a wrinkle in her hand
    So delicate and fine.
And when my chaperon is seen,
    They come from everywhere —
    The dear old boys with silvery hair,
    With old-time grace and old-time air,
To greet their old-time queen.

They bow as my young Midas here
    Will never learn to bow
(The dancing-masters do not teach
    That gracious reverence now);
With voices quavering just a bit,
    They play their old parts through,
    They talk of folk who used to woo,
    Of hearts that broke in 'fifty-two—
Now none the worst for it.

And as those aged crickets chirp
    I watch my chaperon's face,
And see the dear old features take
    A new and tender grace —
And in her happy eyes I see
    Her youth awakening bright,
    With all its hope, desire, delight—
    Ah, me! I wish that I were quite
As young—as young as she!

VIII. A SONG OF BEDFORD STREET

IT 'S a long time ago and a poor time to boast of,
    The foolish old time of two young people's start;
But sweet were the days that young love made the most of—
    So short by the clock, and so long by the heart!
We lived in a cottage in old Greenwich Village,
    With a tiny clay plot that was burnt brown and hard;
But it softened at last to my girl's patient tillage,
    And the roses sprang up in our little back-yard.

The roses sprang up and the yellow day-lilies;
    And heartsease and pansies, sweet Williams and stocks,
And bachelors'-buttons and bright daffodillies
    Filled green little beds that I bordered with box.
They were plain country posies, bright-hued and sweet-smelling,
    And the two of us worked for them, worked long and hard;
And the flowers she had loved in her old-country dwelling,
    They made her at home in our little back-yard.

BALLADS OF THE TOWN

In the morning I dug while the breakfast was cooking,
    And went to the shop, where I toiled all the day;
And at night I returned, and I found my love looking
    With her bright country eyes down the dull city way.
And first she would tell me what flowers were blooming,
    And her soft hand slipped into a hand that was hard,
And she led through the house, till a breeze came perfuming
    Our little back hall from our little back yard.

It was long, long ago, and we have n't grown wealthy;
    And we don't live in state up in Madison Square:
But the old man is hale, and he 's happy and healthy,
    And his wife 's none the worse for the gray in her hair.
Each year lends a sweeter new scent to the roses;
    Each year makes hard life seem a little less hard;
And each year a new love for old lovers discloses —
    Come, wife, let us walk in our little back yard!

LATER LYRICS

THE RED BOX AT VESEY STREET

PAST the Red Box at Vesey street
   Swing two strong tides of hurrying feet,
And up and down and all the day
Rises a sullen roar, to say
The Bowery has met Broadway.
And where the confluent current brawls
Stands, fair and dear and old, St. Paul's,
Through her grand window looking down
Upon the fever of the town;
Rearing her shrine of patriot pride
Above that hungry human-tide
Mad with the lust of sordid gain,
Wild for the things that God holds vain;
Blind, selfish, cruel — Stay there! out
A man is turning from the rout,
And stops to drop a folded sheet
In the Red Box at Vesey street.

LATER LYRICS

On goes he to the money-mart,
A broker, shrewd and tricky-smart;
But in the space you saw him stand,
He reached and grasped a brother's hand:
And some poor bed-rid wretch will find
Bed-life a little less unkind
For that man's stopping. They who pass
Under St. Paul's broad roseate glass
Have but to reach their hands to gain
The pitiful world of prisoned pain.
The hospital's poor captive lies
Waiting the day with weary eyes,
Waiting the day, to hear again
News of the outer world of men,
Brought to him in a crumpled sheet
From the Red Box at Vesey street

For the Red Box at Vesey street
Was made because men's hearts must beat;
Because the humblest kindly thought
May do what wealth has never bought.
That journal in your hand you hold
To you already has grown old,—
Stale, dull, a thing to throw away,—
Yet since the earliest gleam of day

LATER LYRICS

Men in a score of hospitals
Have lain and watched the whitewashed walls;
Waiting the hour that brings more near
The Life so infinitely dear —
The Life of trouble, toil, and strife,
Hard, if you will — but Life, Life, Life!
Tell them, O friend! that life is sweet
Through the Red Box at Vesey street.

SHRIVEN

A. D. 1425

"After he had given his final directions, he asked his physicians how long they thought he might live. And when they told him, 'About two hours,' he shut out from his thoughts every earthly care, and spent his remaining moments in devotion."

I HAVE let the world go.
                      That's the door that closed
Behind the holy father. I am shrived.
All's done — all's said — all's shaped and rounded out —
And one hour yet to wait for death. Good Lord!
How easy 't was to let this vain life go!
Why, I protest, I, who have fought for life
These fifty years more times than I would count,
I gave the poor thing up but now as though
I toss'd away a shilling — ask the priest!
I gave life as lightly as I gave him
For an altar-cloth that scarf of cloth of gold
The King bound round my arm at Agincourt.

   .   .   .   .

LATER LYRICS

One hour—one hour! and then a tug o' the heart
And I shall see the saints. How plain they make it,
These honest men of God! Was it at Lisle
I met that paunchy little yellow friar,
Like Cupid in a cassock with the jaundice,
And played at cards with him two days together?
Stay, 'twas at Calais, where I fought the Count—
By 'r Lady, but they mock'd him!—'twas at Calais—
Now had I had some converse with that brother
It might have been the better for my soul.
Though 'tis all one, I take it, now. . . . The Abbess!
He told a master-story of an Abbess—
An Abbess and a Clerk—but godly talk,
If I remember me aright . . . we had not.

. . . .

Ay, 'tis fair lying here, to watch the sun
Creep up yon wall. I would that I had thought
To give that priest the ruby in my hilt
To buy him better store of sacred oil—
The anointed go to Paradise, methinks,
Something too rancid-flavored.
      What's the clock?
This hour's too full of minutes—minutes—minutes.
Ah, well, I have done with time. 'Tis but an hour.
I have let go the world.
      Would my dog were here!

SONG FOR LABOR DAY[6]

HIS voice who made the land
  For his holiest hath decreed it;
His chosen it shall stand
  And the Lord shall lead it.

  Work, work, thy lot shall be,
And the worker shall possess thee —
  Grown strong from sea to sea,
No foeman shall distress thee —
  Work on! Work on! America!

His voice in that day said:
  "Thou shalt labor, O my chosen,
When suns are hot o'erhead;
  When waters shall be frozen.

Work, work, thy lot shall be,
And the worker shall possess thee —
Grown strong from sea to sea,
No foeman shall distress thee —
Work on! Work on! America!

His voice hath spoken down:
"Thou shalt conquer the despoiler:
Thy labor is thy crown
And thy might, O Toiler!"

Work, work, thy lot shall be,
And the worker shall possess thee —
Grown strong from sea to sea,
No foeman shall distress thee —
Work on! Work on! America!

AN OLD SONG

[THE SONG OF SOLOMON, V. 2, 5]

LOVE, I have wandered a weary way,
    A weary way for thee,
The East is wan with the smile of the day—
    Open thy door to me!

My hair is wet with the dew of the night
    That falls from the cedar-tree;
The shadows are dark; but the East is light—
    Open thy door to me!

The stones of the road have bruised my feet—
    The hours till morn are three—
Thou that hast spikenard precious sweet,
    Open thy door to me!

Stay not thy hand upon the lock,
    Nor thy fingers on the key.
In the breeze before morn the tree-tops rock—
    Open thy door to me!

LATER LYRICS

My love is the fairest, the only one,
  The choice of her house is she—
The height of the heaven hath seen the sun—
  Open thy door to me!

The holy kiss of my lips and thine
  Shall the sun have grace to see?
The hours foregone of the night are nine—
  Open thy door to me!

UNAWARE

I WOULD not have you so kindly
  Thus early in friendship's year—
A little too gently, blindly,
  You let me near.

So long as my voice is duly
  Calm as a friend's should be,
In my eyes the hunger unruly
  You will not see.

The eyes that you lift so brightly,
  Frankly to welcome mine—
You bend them again as lightly
  And note no sign.

I had rather your pale cheek reddened
  With the flush of an angry pride—
That a look with disliking deadened
  My gaze defied.

If so in the Spring's full season
  Your glance should soften and fall,
When, reckless with fever's unreason,
  I tell you all.

THE QUEST

UPON my lips there fell, when first the Night
    Pales in the highest heaven, seeing Day
  Far down the fathomless Eastern depths away—
Pales with a fearful joy, a dread delight—
Upon my lips, with wakeful watching white,
    There fell a kiss. One instant's space it lay
    Soft as a rose-leaf that the West-winds fray,
And then my eyes awoke to dazzled sight.

The warmth, the tender impact and the thrill
    Burnt on my lips, and the calm pulse of Sleep
      Awoke and quivered quick in soft surprise.
From that day forward knew I Love!
                            And still
    By day I search, and nightly vigil keep
      For Her revealed to me in such strange wise.

LUTETIA

1856

OFTEN in visions of the night I seem
    To pace thy avenues with enchanted feet;
Walk thy broad boulevards from the mid-day heat
Till myriad gas-jets through the calm dusk gleam;
See moonlight crown Napoleon's tower supreme;
    Watch in the Latin Quarter's darkest street
    From revelling in some cavernous retreat,
Strange student-shapes into the cool night stream—
Young hungry gods of genius—or where beam
    Lights of Lampsakian gardens: where is blown
    White hot the fire of folly, to turn again.
Yet ever flies the spirit of my dream
    To that high garret, where, sick, blind, alone,
    Lies Heine on his pallet-prison of pain.

THE HEART OF THE TREE

AN ARBOR-DAY SONG

WHAT does he plant who plants a tree?
   He plants the friend of sun and sky;
He plants the flag of breezes free;
   The shaft of beauty, towering high;
   He plants a home to heaven anigh
     For song and mother-croon of bird
     In hushed and happy twilight heard—
The treble of heaven's harmony—
These things he plants who plants a tree.

What does he plant who plants a tree?
   He plants cool shade and tender rain,
And seed and bud of days to be,
   And years that fade and flush again;
   He plants the glory of the plain;
     He plants the forest's heritage;
     The harvest of a coming age;
The joy that unborn eyes shall see—
These things he plants who plants a tree.

LATER LYRICS

What does he plant who plants a tree?
  He plants, in sap and leaf and wood,
In love of home and loyalty
  And far-cast thought of civic good—
  His blessing on the neighborhood
    Who in the hollow of His hand
    Holds all the growth of all our land—
A nation's growth from sea to sea
Stirs in his heart who plants a tree.

"THEY ALSO SERVE"

A POEM READ BEFORE THE ARMY OF THE POTOMAC AT ITS TWENTY-SIXTH ANNUAL REUNION, NEW LONDON, CONN., JUNE 18, 1895

FRIENDS — for we are all friends in one great bond —
That, born in death, shall go death's power beyond,
That shall endure so long as love shall twine
The first Spring blossoms for the patriot shrine.
So long as men shall deck with living green
The dust of friends unknown, unmet, unseen;
So long as Love shall quicken Memory's birth,
Each year to seek the consecrated earth,
To wreathe the tombs among the fresh Spring showers,
With heaven's own banner and with earth's own flowers —
So long the sacred tie that makes us kin
Shall know no petty bonds of time or space,
But hold us in the friendship of one race —
The friendship that our dead have knit us in.

LATER LYRICS

Here I am come to speak to you, my brothers —
My elder brothers — of a long-passed day
When you were fighting for this flag; when others
Remained at home to watch — to yearn — to pray.
What shall I tell to you, who truly followed
The troublous path my young soul longed to go?
You know that for your help God's palm was hollowed,
And how his strength prevailed against the foe.
But, may I tell the tale of those who waited
Patient at home — the old, the infirm, the young —
Watching the strife wherein they were not fated
Even to die unhonored and unsung?

    What does the boy do who goes to bed
    In the great third year of the war,
    With the farm-house roof hanging low over head,
    And the path of the moon stretching out before,
    Out over the wood and over the lake,
    To the dusty highway the soldiers take
    When they march on their way to the South?

    What does he do when he goes to bed? —
    He lays on the pillow a touzled head,
    And the tired eyelids that all the day
    Have been with the face of the world at play;

LATER LYRICS

Watching the birds and the swing of the trees,
Watching the chipmunks more quick than the breeze,
Watching the melons a taking on green,
Watching the myriad things to be seen —

— They close for a moment and open again,
For he hears the tramp of the marching men
Southward and ever south;
And he swallows a sob, and shuts tight his mouth,
And orders his heart to the right-about,
But even in slumber his tears slip out,
That the sound of the drum and the fife
Is slipping away to the strife,
Where he may not go
Till sun and snow
Have carried his eager young spirit — say —
A couple of years on its patriot way.

Oh, how he yearns for it,
How his heart burns for it —
How the shrill music of drum and of fife
Thrills through the whole of him,
Wakes the young soul of him —
Oh, to be with them and pay with his life!

LATER LYRICS

What does the boy do who goes to bed
In the great third year of the war?
Wakes in the morn when the east is red,
And the west is silvered o'er;
Wakes in the morning and goes to work,
Eating his heart, but too proud to shirk,
Dropping the corn in the heart of the hill,
Plying his spade and his hoe with a will;
And his mother looks from the kitchen stoop,
With reddened eyelids that quiver and droop,
At the one boy left her — O, friends in blue —
Was n't he fighting as well as you?

Oh, let me not by any doubtful word
Question your mighty service: what you wrought
Was wrought forever, and the eternal years
Shall not undo it. But we all have seen
The glory of that mighty miracle.

The foulest of foul stains you washed with blood
From off your country's shield: your strong hand rent
The chains ourselves had forged ourselves to fetter,
But, oh! remember that no fleshly wound
Fell crueler than the blows the true hearts bore
You left behind you when you took your way.

LATER LYRICS

Do you know how they looked in our eyes, do you know how they looked as they went? —
The picture is ever before me — friends, will you look at yourselves?

See how they swing down the street with the glint of the sun
Silvering the steel of the gun.
With an easy swing to the hips, as they march on, shoulder to shoulder,
Doubtful, uncertain at first, and then growing firmer and bolder
As the cheers of the crowd rise round them, and run in a rattling roar
Down on each side of the column and out like a fire before.
It swells by their side to a thunder that hushes the beat of their feet,
It catches their cadence of marching and rolls it ahead down the street;
Down the whole length of the roadway, through the throng of the thousands that wait,
Down goes the heralding thunder as the troops march on in state.
And down where the Battery breezes are blowing through Bowling Green

LATER LYRICS

The men of New York are cheering the troops that they have not seen.
Oh, glorious pageant of war that shall sweep you along amid cheers! —
But the wife you have left is this moment thanking God for the blindness of tears.

She kissed you, and she raised unclouded eyes
That hid the unspeakable pain of unshed tears.
She kissed you and she lifted up your child,
For she had taught him to be brave like you —
Or her — how shall we put it, O, my friend?
She kissed you, and she sent you on your way,
Her noble wifehood strengthening you for fight,
And turned her patient face toward home to stay
And bear the wound that aches from morn to night.
Oh, trust me if I speak of those who shared
Your pain and not your glory; it is not
To rob your laurels of a single leaf,
But to proclaim how that close tie of grief
Bound you in bonds of love to childish hearts
That in these days, grown closer to the age
Of those they honor, still recall the past —
Recall the past, and how you met the task
You found set for you, and not newly set,

LATER LYRICS

But waiting for the work of men like you,
But waiting for the faith of men like you —
Waiting through centuries of wrong and shame
Since Christ decreed the brotherhood of Man,
For it was as His soldiers that they went,
Who, being dead, have left their trust to us.

I was not of you, but that tie still binds
My childish memories unto unborn minds,
And I shall teach *my* boy the way to go
By paths your fearless footsteps served to show.
And if he serves his country firm and true,
'T is that his father learned to serve from *you*.

NOTES

NOTES

¹ "There was a vague murmur in the air of little brooks, that one might fancy had lost their way in the darkness, and were whispering together how they should get home."
———— "In the Distance," by G. P. Lathrop.

² The only authority I have for calling this "A Real Romance" is the following, clipped from a stray newspaper in '77 or '78 :

"A school-girl at Bellefontaine, Ohio, offended her boy lover, and he refused to speak to her. She passed a note to him, asking forgiveness, but he refused. She wrote to him again, saying that she would kill herself if he did not make up; and he replied that he would be glad to go to her funeral. She then began her suicidal efforts by drinking a bottle of red ink, which only made her sick. A bottle of black ink had no deadlier effect. Finally, she cut her throat with a knife, but not fatally, though she made a deep and dangerous gash."

³ Like the Roman citizen's right of appeal to Cæsar, there was, according to some authorities, a supreme right of appeal to Harold of Normandy. It was invoked by crying "Haro! Haro! Haro!" In a modified form, the legal tradition still survives, I believe, in some of the Channel Islands.

⁴ Read at the farewell dinner to Salvini, New-York, April 26th, 1883.

⁵ The sun of Tubby Hook has set.
'T is *INWOOD* now — and folks forget.

⁶ Written for Franklin Public School, Labor Day, 1894.

www.ingramcontent.com/pod-product-compliance
Lightning Source LLC
Chambersburg PA
CBHW031947230426
43672CB00010B/2073